Action Planning

Action Planning

**How to use planning weekends
and urban design action teams
to improve your environment.**

Compiled and edited by
Nick Wates

Foreword by
HRH The Prince of Wales

Published in association with the
Urban Villages Forum

With the generous support of
English Partnerships and
Inner City Aid

The Prince of Wales's Institute of Architecture

Action Planning

Compiler and Editor: Nick Wates.
Editorial Board: Ros Tennyson, John Thompson, Nick Wates.
Photographs: John Thompson and Nick Wates unless otherwise stated.
Design and production: Jeremy Brook, Graphic Ideas, Hastings.

Published 1996 by The Prince of Wales's Institute of Architecture,
14 Gloucester Gate, London NW1 4HG, tel 0171 916 7380, fax 0171 916 7381,
in association with the Urban Villages Forum and with the generous support of
English Partnerships and Inner City Aid.

Printed on chlorine-free paper by Weald Press, St Leonards-on-Sea, East Sussex.

ISBN 1 898465 11 8

*Freestanding quotations are from written statements or from interviews by the
editor unless otherwise indicated.*

Cover photograph: *Team review session at Poundbury Planning Weekend, 1989.*

Frontispiece: *Plenary session at Wornington Green Planning Weekend, 1989.*

Contents

Acknowledgements

This handbook has been produced as part of the Tools for Community Design programme which is supported by The Prince of Wales's Institute of Architecture (POWIA). The programme has been developed by Nick Wates in association with Ros Tennyson and John Thompson under the guidance of the Institute's Director of Research, Professor Keith Critchlow and Director, Dr Richard John.

The editor would like to acknowledge in particular the work of the American Institute of Architects whose programme of Regional & Urban Design Assistance Teams (R/UDATs) pioneered the Action Planning approach. Special thanks are also due to Jeremy Caulton for his invaluable thesis on the transferability of the technique, English Partnerships and Inner City Aid for providing financial support and all those who provided material, participated in the 'Editing Day' or commented on drafts. They include:

Mel Agace, *Practical Projects Co-ordinator, POWIA.*
Jon Allen, *Research Co-ordinator, POWIA.*
Sultan Barakat, *Director, Post-war Reconstruction and Development Unit, Institute of Architectural Studies, York.*
Michael Baynes, *Development Surveyor, Hawk Development Management plc.*
John Billingham, *Editor, Urban Design Quarterly.*
Jeff Bishop, *Director, BDOR Ltd.*
Jeremy Brook, *Graphic Ideas.*
Jeremy Caulton, *Senior Consultant, Urban Initiatives.*
Caroline Clark, *Regeneration Unit, Civic Trust.*
Rob Cowan, *writer and consultant on urban affairs.*
Keith Critchlow, *Director of Research, POWIA.*
Alastair Dick-Cleland, *student, POWIA.*
Peter Eley, *Architect.*
Nicholas Falk, *Director, URBED urban & economic development group.*
Richard Feilden, *Chairman, Community Architecture Group, Royal Institute of British Architects.*
Tony Gibson, *consultant.*
Rod Hackney, *Chairman, Inner City Aid.*
Gail Hallyburton, *Urban Villages Forum.*
Nancy Haque, *Professional Firms Group, Business in the Community.*
Nabeel Hamdi, *Director, Centre for Development & Emergency Planning, Oxford Brookes University.*
Sue Hargreaves, *John Thompson & Partners.*

Brian Hanson, *Director, The Prince of Wales's Project Office.*
Lorraine Hart, *Research and Development Officer, The Environment Trust.*
Ian Haywood, *Ian Haywood Partnership.*
Amanda Heslop, *Training Officer, Help Age International.*
Richard John, *Director, POWIA.*
Joan Kean, *Project Director, Newcastle Architecture Workshop.*
Charles Knevitt, *Director, Polymath.*
Chris Lakin, *Director, Inner City Aid.*
Caroline Lwin, *Architect.*
David Lewis, *American Institute of Architects.*
Arnold Linden, *Planning Advisory Group, Royal Institute of British Architects.*
Charmian Marshall, *Urban Villages Forum.*
Guy Oliver, *student, POWIA.*
Jenneth Parker, *education consultant.*
Richard Pullen, *Department of the Environment.*
Debbie Radcliffe, *administrator and actress.*
Mark Rasmussen, *Researcher, POWIA.*
Stephen Reinke, *President, London Chapter, American Institute of Architects.*
Jon Rowland, *Chairman, Urban Design Group.*
Jane Samuels, *student, POWIA.*
Claire Scott, *Research Administrator, POWIA.*
Louise Scott, *arts organiser.*
Alan Simpson, *Urban Design Associates.*
Sukhvinder Stubbs, *Community Development Manager, English Partnerships.*
David Taylor, *Chief Executive, English Partnerships.*
Ros Tennyson, *Community Development Consultant, Partnership Unit, Prince of Wales Business Leaders Forum.*
John Thompson, *John Thompson & Partners.*
John F C Turner, *Architect and writer.*
David Turrent, *Architect, ECD architects.*
Richard Twinch, *Senior Tutor, POWIA.*
Upkar Ubhi, *student, POWIA.*
Max and Mae Wates, *children.*
Ted Watts, *Chairman, Watts & Partners.*
David Wilcox, *Director, Partnership.*
John Worthington, *Director, Institute of Advanced Architectural Studies, University of York, Deputy Chairman, DEGW.*
Charles Zucker, *Director, Community Design & Development, American Institute of Architects.*

Workshop at an 'Editing Day' held at The Prince of Wales's Institute of Architecture in February 1995. Thirty-three practitioners, designers, editors and potential readers helped to shape this book using felt-tip pens on wall mounted page blow-ups; a process adapted from Action Planning itself. Participants also took steps to improve the co-ordination of Action Planning support frameworks. An Action Planning Task Group, with representatives from several national organisations, has been set up to continue this work.

ST. JAMES'S PALACE

Over the last few years I have come to admire greatly the impact and success of a particular approach to Community Architecture known as Action Planning. In Britain, including both Scotland and Northern Ireland, and in other parts of the world, including Germany, I have been greatly impressed and heartened to see the energy and commitment that can be generated by this technique, which brings together interested people from all walks of life and gives them the opportunity over a number of days to discuss in detail ways to improve their built environment. It is a refreshing contrast to the conventional bureaucratic approach to planning, as local authorities and government agencies in countries throughout the world are beginning to discover.

It is essential to find the means to help local people and specialists of every kind to work creatively together in this way if we are to build better and more sustainable communities where people can live in greater harmony with their surroundings. Carefully structured Action Plannning events are a promising, and increasingly proven, way of encouraging this. They can be relevant anywhere at any stage of the development process. They can be useful for exploring the future of a single site, a neighbourhood, a town, or even an entire region. Equally, they can be used to explore the impact of new legislation or other factors involving change.

The practice - and art - of Action Planning is still very new. I am delighted that my Institute of Architecture is publishing this first handbook to help people grasp the immense opportunities offered by this valuable technique.

HRH The Prince of Wales taking part in an Action Planning event at Poundbury, Dorchester, 1989. Over 2000 people attended the 5-day 'planning weekend' to explore the implications of building a new town on Duchy of Cornwall property. Over 75% of the 400 people who filled in a questionnaire thought the event worthwhile and almost 90% wanted continued involvement as the project progressed.

Introduction

How do you go about improving your city or neighbourhood? How can you make it more useful, enjoyable and sustainable?

'Action Planning' could be the start of an answer. By organising an 'Action Planning event', you may be able to come up with some visionary new ideas and, just as important, ways of implementing them.

Action Planning is a new technique of urban management which has already been practised to great effect. Instead of relying solely on private initiative and bureaucratic planning procedures, strategies for action are generated by getting all interested parties to work together at carefully structured events - normally lasting 4 or 5 days - guided by a multidisciplinary team of independent specialists.

It must be stressed that Action Planning is only one of many 'community planning' techniques available. Others - such as 'Planning for Real' or establishing a community design centre or development trust - can be integrated with it or used as alternatives. There are also many variations within the Action Planning formula itself. You will have to assess:

- whether an Action Planning event is the right technique for your particular situation and, if so;

- what type and scale of event would be most appropriate.

Working through this book will help you make an assessment.

Organised well, Action Planning events can be immensely rewarding and a valuable addition to conventional planning. Organised badly, they can be a sad waste of energy. As with all such techniques, the process is open to abuse unless good practice principles are followed.

This handbook has therefore been produced to allow people to benefit from experience gained so far. It is for anyone wanting to improve their surroundings and particularly for those taking part in, or organising, events. It focusses on the popular 5-day events spanning a weekend, but the same basic principles apply to shorter or longer events. The advice can easily be adjusted accordingly.

The book has been designed to be useful before, during and after events. Double-page spreads are self-contained and include handy sample documents and checklists with space for your own additions. Pages can be blown up to create exhibition panels or reduced to form leaflets or working documents.

Beware though of copying too slavishly. An important part of the process is devising your own process. Use the book as a guide and stimulant, not an instruction manual.

This is the first edition and it is still early days in the evolution of Action Planning. Comments from readers and feedback from events would be most welcome for compiling future editions. Please send to:

The Editor, Action Planning,
The Prince of Wales's Institute of Architecture,
14 Gloucester Gate,
London NW1 4HG.

Using this book

Checklists. Use these to plan your own events.

Sample Documents. Use these (modified) to save time.

PRINCIPLES

- The essential ingredients. Ignore these at your peril.

TIPS

- Good ideas (hopefully) based on a bit of experience.

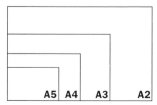

Copy pages as leaflets or exhibition posters.

"I only went to be nosy. I just went to see what was going on and before I knew what had happened I was in the thick of it. I went Friday, Saturday, went back Sunday for an hour or two and then Monday night as well. I thought it was brilliant. I really enjoyed it. Very hard work but really exciting. It took me a week to sleep properly afterwards; all these ideas were springing back into my head and I was going through them one at a time. What made the weekend so good was having professional people there with local people as well. That was the ideal combination. Having everybody in one room together slogging it out got a lot of good ideas out."

Donna Fallows, resident, West Silvertown, London, speaking after the West Silvertown Community Planning Weekend, December 1993 (shown above with baby).

Section 1
Overview

Context

New approach.
Interdisciplinary, collaborative and community-based planning.

"If more towns, villages and cities held regular, cathartic events which examined what exactly was happening to their citizens' habitat and attempted to seek solutions which met with the broad approval of the public through a process which mixed professional, public and private interests we would have, I think, a much better country – one where the rejection of the architect would not be automatic and the dead hand of professional planning would be removed."

Lee Mallet,
Editor,
Building Design,
Editorial, 4 November 1994.

*R/UDAT Handbook, page 84.

Action Planning has not suddenly been invented. Rather, the technique has evolved – and is still evolving – from practical experience in many parts of the world. It can best be seen as part of an emerging technology of 'community planning' or 'community architecture'; approaches which make it easier for people to participate in the creation and management of their built environment.

The underlying philosophy of Action Planning is interdisciplinary, collaborative and community-based. The assumption is that better environments can be created if local communities take the driving seat and work closely and directly with a wide range of specialists. In arriving at the fairly sophisticated process described in this book, practitioners have drawn on experience from many disciplines including company management, human psychology and urban design.

As a clearly defined planning technique, Action Planning events lasting 4 or 5 days (the main focus of this book) were pioneered almost 30 years ago in the United States. Over one-tenth of that nation's population is now estimated to have benefited from over 125 events in a programme run by the American Institute of Architects alone.* Other national, state and local institutions are also increasingly promoting similar activity.

During the last decade, Action Planning has surfaced in Europe. The American approach has been adapted to the different cultural conditions and fused with European regeneration experience.

Over 25 'planning weekends' and 'urban design action team' events lasting 4 or 5 days have now

ACTION PLANNING NICK WATES

been held in Europe, mostly in the UK. At the same time a variety of related initiatives have evolved, ranging from 1-day 'design charrettes' to urban design 'task forces' lasting several weeks.

As yet Action Planning has not been part of the statutory planning process. The initiative for events has come mostly from professional institutions and practitioners keen to explore more creative methods. Developers, community organisations and local authorities have become willing supporters as they seized the opportunity to work positively with the other groups involved. Recently there has been increasing interest from national government which has begun to see the economic and social benefits that can result. The possibility of legislation to incorporate Action Planning in the statutory planning process has begun to be discussed seriously.

In the meantime, events continue to be organised on an ad-hoc basis and the number of enthusiasts grows. An extraordinary feature of the Action Planning phenomenon is the way that people who have experienced it become convinced of its value.

There is still much experimenting and evaluation needed. But those involved in the development of this new activity are confident it will come to play a major role in the future planning and management of human settlements. Whether they are right, and precisely what that role might be, remains to be seen.

Uses for Action Planning

- **City futures**
  Devising new visions for the future of a city or region.

- **Revival strategies**
  Developing strategies for declining industrial or inner city areas.

- **Agenda 21 strategies**
  Developing Local 'Agenda 21' strategies for sustainable development.

- **Traffic solutions**
  Resolving congestion problems in historic town centres or exploring new transport route options.

- **Site proposals**
  Devising and testing development proposals for empty sites or redundant buildings.

- **Design ideas**
  Exploring options for design improvements to historic buildings.

- **New towns**
  Exploring the best way of building major new settlements or integrating new development with old.

- **Development plans**
  Involving the public in the early stages of preparing statutory development plans.

Key features of Action Planning

There are several types of Action Planning event and a variety of labels have been used to describe them. Common features are:

- **Intensive work sessions**
  A fast-paced, intensive programme of work sessions – normally lasting from 4 to 5 days – is preceded by months of careful organisation and followed by practical action and evaluation. Often the event spans a weekend.

- **Community participation**
  The driving force for the event comes from within the community and everyone affected is encouraged to be involved.

- **Broad mission**
  All the problems and opportunities of a particular site, a neighbourhood, a city or even a region are examined in a holistic manner with a minimum of preconceptions.

- **Multidisciplinary work process**
  People from all the relevant disciplines and trades work closely together in a hands-on, non-hierarchical fashion.

- **Independent facilitators**
  Events are normally facilitated by a Team of people with no direct involvement in the area or direct vested interest. This helps provide a neutral forum for debate and confidence in the outcome.

"I cannot think of another opportunity where such lengthy meetings can take place amongst experts in their own fields discussing issues to their bitter conclusion. This is incredibly stimulating since thought processes build on themselves exponentially and realistic solutions to seemingly impossible problems become apparent."

**Michael Baynes,
Development Surveyor,
Hawk Development
Management plc,**
6 December 1993.

16

- **High profile**
  Events are highly publicised to ensure that everyone has the opportunity to get involved and that the results are widely disseminated. They normally end with a public presentation and written report.

- **Flexibility**
  The process can easily be adjusted to suit the needs of each particular community.

Typical Outcomes

- Visions for an area's future.
- Agreed objectives.
- Agendas for action.
- Proposals for a particular site or programme.
- Suggestions for organisational changes.
- Achievable targets.
- Local coalitions and leadership.

Holistic.
Vision for a new urban village in London's docklands conceived and drawn up during an Action Planning event. Top: site as existing. (West Silvertown, 1993.)

Benefits of Action Planning

Action Planning can achieve objectives which are hard to achieve in any other way. These include:

- **Creation of shared visions** for a community's future and identification of long- and short-term strategies for implementing them.

- **Catalyst for action** of all kinds by releasing blockages in the development process.

- **Resolution of complex problems** or at least a clearer identification of issues and goals.

- **Revitalisation of local networks** for community development.

- **Fostering of consensus building** among different interest groups leading to better integration.

- **Promotion of urban design capability** of local agencies and improvement of environmental standards.

- **Heightened public awareness** of development issues resulting from the provision of an open forum for debate.

- **Morale boost** for all those involved as a result of experiencing team working.

"Action planning can be extremely successful both in galvanising community participation and allowing collective decisions to be made in an efficient and effective way. An Action Planning event that has been properly designed has the ability to create a unique chemistry of activity and energy, bringing together all the potential players working towards a common goal, and with the ability to produce new and sometimes unexpected results in a more effective way than by using conventional professional methods alone."

John Thompson,
Chairman,
John Thompson & Partners,
7 February 1995.

Action Planning should NOT be seen as:

- A substitute for a statutory planning framework.

- A substitute for long-term participatory programmes.

- A technique for consultation only; it is essentially a participatory process.

- A way of replacing the services of local professionals and/or officials.

- A way of imposing ideas on a community from outside.

Shared visions.
Getting public, private and voluntary sectors to move in the same direction. (Cartoon by Louis Hellman, depicting the main stakeholders – development corporation, landowners, local authority, developers, local community – at West Silvertown Community Planning Weekend, 1993.)

Typical Products

Immediate
- A set of proposals for action set out in:
  - a broadsheet and press release.
  - an illustrated report.
  - an exhibition.
  - a slide show.

Short term
- Local steering committees to build on the event's work.
- Periodic progress reports.

Long term
- Ongoing programme of activities.
- Evaluation of the impact of the event.

Why Action Planning works

Action Planning 'works' because the process combines a unique mix of ingredients which respond to the complexity of today's development issues:

- **Open community involvement**
  There is scope for all members of the community to participate in a wide variety of ways. This can lead to a new sense of cohesion and consensus on goals, to the formation of new partnerships and to the development of a sense of equity.

- **Creative working methods**
  Professionals of all disciplines work in a hands-on manner with each other and with non-professionals in a neutral environment. This breaks down conventional professional boundaries and creates a chemistry between people which can be magnetic; releasing spirit, humour, imagination, positive thinking and collective creativity.

- **Dynamism**
  The carefully structured, defined timetable creates a focus of public attention and provides deadlines for results. A critical mass of activity is generated which is hard to ignore.

- **Fresh thinking**
  The independent Team provides an opportunity for new ideas to be put forward which can overcome past divisions and indecision. Proposals emerge which nobody would ever have imagined.

"I know from my own experience that Action Planning can create a shared vision for regeneration and bring innovative solutions from the people who have to live with the effects. It instills a sense of ownership ensuring that the outcomes are more sustainable."

David Taylor,
Chief Executive,
English Partnerships,
15 February 1995.

- **Visual approach**
  The use of urban design techniques of drawing and model-making provides an easily accessible way for people to think about, and communicate, visions for their community's future.

- **Realism**
  The process addresses both the physical and natural environment as they are, rather than the abstract concepts which tend to result from specialism and departmentalism. The inhabitants' own concerns are placed on the agenda.

Unique chemistry.
Professionals, local residents, politicians and developers take time off for group photographs (Cape Hill, Sandwell, 1990; Poundbury, 1989 and West Silvertown, 1993).

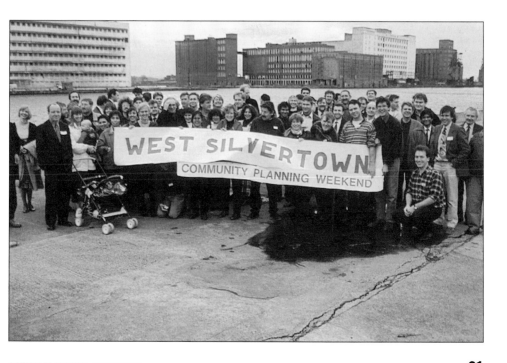

Action Planning process

Who does what and when

	Getting Started ▶ 1–2 months*
Local Interests **Individuals and** **organisations**	• Concern to improve environment. • Stimulate action. • Establish Steering Group and Host (see below).
Steering Group/ **Host/Organiser** **Main enthusiasts and** **technical advisors**	• Formation/appointment. • Explore options for action. • Prepare proposal. • Stimulate enthusiasm. • Secure commitment from all affected parties. • Raise funds. • Commitment to proceed.
Event Team **Specialists from** **complementary** **disciplines**	
Support Bodies **National, international** **and regional organisations**	• Supply general information and advice. • Evaluation visit if requested

"It's a fantastic way of putting a major scheme together and could revolutionise the way we do development. It could be a blueprint for putting major commercial schemes together."

Barry Wick, developer,
London & Edinburgh Trust plc,
Building Design,
3 February 1989.

*Timescales.
Action Planning events can be of varying lengths but the process remains more or less the same. The length of the event and the lead times will be determined by the nature of the issues faced and the extent and capacity of existing local networks. Timescales

Preparation ▶	The Event ▶	Follow-up ▶
2–4 months*	several days*	ongoing*
• Build momentum, enthusiasm and expectation through discussion and by focussing attention on the main issues.	• Participate in public sessions.	• Analyse proposals. • Develop support for strategies and projects. • Apply pressure for implementation. • Ongoing participation.
• Select Team Chairperson, Team members, Advisors and consultants. • Establish administration and technical support. • Gather information. • Prepare venues. • Publicise.	• Event management and administration.	• Assess proposals and prioritise. • Agree plan of action. • Publicity. • Spearhead and co-ordinate. implementation. • Maintain momentum.
• Homework on the locality and the Action Planning process. • Reconnaissance visit by Chairperson.	• Arrive. • Reconnaissance. • Briefings. • Topic workshops. • Design workshops. • Brainstorm. • Prepare proposals. • Presentation. • Leave.	• Revisit and assist as requested.
• Supply detailed information and contacts.	• Observe. • Participate. • Assist if asked.	• Monitor and evaluate. • Assist if asked.

shown above have been found to be the most effective for major urban design issues of, say, a neighbourhood or city. Shorter events work well for simpler issues such as making proposals for a single site. Shorter lead times are possible where local networks are well developed. Longer lead times can be useful for building community capacity.

Community participation. *Staged publicity photograph organised by Hulme Regeneration Ltd with local schoolchildren in 1992. The aim was to generate publicity for, and encourage participation in, a community planning weekend to create a strategic masterplan for the physical, social and economic regeneration of an inner city neighbourhood in Manchester.*

Section 2

Getting started

Taking the plunge

So you think you want to hold an Action Planning event? Congratulations. But here's a list of 10 things you should check out before making a definite decision:

1 Read right through this handbook to make sure you understand what will be involved. Check out other sources (see *Publications* page 84).

2 Discuss it informally with people who have done it before and organisations that might provide support (see *Addresses* page 86).

3 Form a Steering Group to coordinate the event. This should reflect the community's diversity and include all main enthusiasts and key players.

4 Think through what kind of event is likely to be most suitable for the specific issues you face and who might act as Host and Organiser.

5 Think through whether to hold an event under the umbrella of a regional, national or even international organisation. This can provide clout and experience (see *Support Bodies* page 30).

6 Write a 'mission statement' setting out the objectives and how and by whom they are going to be achieved (see samples on next page).

7 Prepare budget estimates and funding strategy (see *Funding* page 32).

8 Approach key representatives of the main interested local parties to get their support.

9 Ask yourselves, do you have, or can you be sure of getting:
- ☐ broad local support?
- ☐ keen Steering Group, Host and Organiser?
- ☐ enough funding or support in kind?
- ☐ clear and achievable mission statement?
- ☐ capability to follow up afterwards?

10 If the answer is yes, **go for it**.

"The huge amount of effort invested in this weekend has paid dividends. The event has not only resulted in a coherent vision for Hulme 5 (housing estate), but has also shifted entrenched attitudes and ploughed through prejudice. Hulme will never be the same again – and neither will those who attended."

Lesley Whitehouse,
Chief Executive,
Hulme Regeneration Ltd,
quoted in event report,
November 1992.

Sample Mission Statements

New Visions for Anytown

Anytown is suffering from a number of difficulties caused by the decline of traditional industries and lack of investment for housing maintenance.

There is high unemployment, homelessness, a number of derelict sites in the town centre and a general sense of uncertainty and despondence.

Several solutions have been put forward over recent years but little action has taken place because of lack of agreement on priorities and lack of funds.

It is proposed to organise an Action Planning event next Spring. The objective is to create a new sense of vision for the town by inviting all members of the community to explore possible options with a Team of specialists from elsewhere. A programme of long- and short-term action will be drawn up. A four-day event is proposed spanning the weekend before Easter. This fits in well with the town council's deadline for a response to developers' proposals for some of the town centre derelict sites and a conference a month later on how to implement Local Agenda 21.

The event is being organised by the Anytown Environment Network in association with the National Urban Trust. It is supported by Anytown Council and the Anytown Chamber of Commerce. Sponsors include Shell and Greenpeace. Architects Company, which has considerable experience of Action Planning, will be engaged to provide the administration and a technical support team will be provided by Anytown College Urban Design Department. The National Urban Trust will assist with assembling the Team of specialists and will monitor progress after the event has taken place.

Anyvillage Traffic Management

Increased traffic in Anyvillage is causing problems for residents and traders alike. Parking is hard to find and there have been several unpleasant incidents involving abuse and even violence on one occasion. Proposals by the local planning department for new car parks have been widely opposed.

Anyvillage parish council proposes to hold a one-day Action Planning Event to thrash out some options. The event will take place during the day and evening to ensure that everyone who wants to has an opportunity to take part. A Team of transport and urban design specialists will facilitate the event and make recommendations. In preparing for the event, the parish council is being assisted by the village school, which is making a model, and officers from the county council planning department. Support and advice is also being provided by the national Civic Trust.

Organisation

**Anytown Action
Planning Weekend**
4-8 April 1996

Action Planning events may be initiated by any individual or organisation. Once the idea has taken root there are various organisational models but most fit within a standard framework (shown diagrammatically opposite).

Organised by Anytown Environment Network in association with the National Urban Trust

Supported by Anytown Town Council and Anytown Chamber of Commerce

Sponsored by Shell and Greenpeace

***Building partnerships.**
Producing a sheet of notepaper is a good way to think through how to position the event.*

PRINCIPLES

- Existing participation mechanisms should be built on but a new single-minded mechanism should be created with complete freedom of action.

- Ultimate responsibility for hosting the event should be taken by a single organisation but this will often be on behalf of a partnership of relevant interests, usually formalised as a Steering Group. The Host may appoint a professional organiser and/or administrator.

- A Team of independent specialists should be appointed to take responsibility for facilitating the event and making recommendations. The Team may be from a regular consultancy or be specially handpicked. Members may be paid or unpaid.*

* It is common practice, particularly in America, for Team members to receive expenses only and to agree not to accept commissions arising from their recommendations. But the process is also increasingly becoming part of standard professional workpractice with Team members being paid fees accordingly. Both approaches have their strengths. The important thing is to have clear and open policies.

- The Team Chairperson should be carefully selected. He or she may wish to work with a core group with previous experience of working together. During the event itself, the Team Chairperson should be in sole charge.

TIPS

- Invite non independent specialists (eg local planners and community leaders) to participate as Advisors not Team members. Otherwise the validity of the recommendations may be jeopardised.

Organisation framework

Working arrangements for an Action Planning event

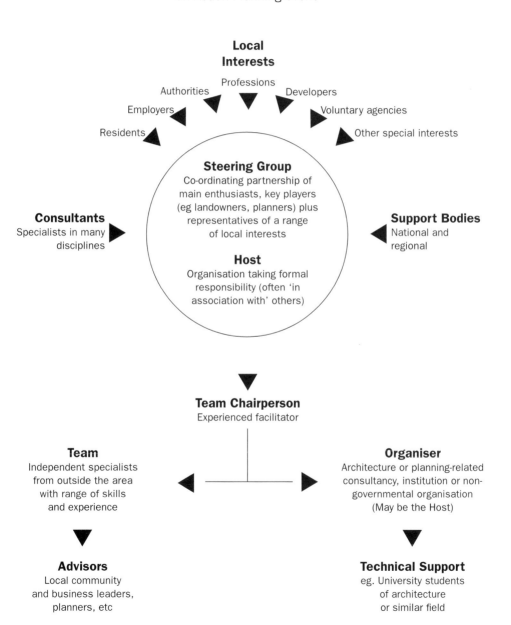

Local Interests

Professions

Authorities

Developers

Employers

Voluntary agencies

Residents

Other special interests

Steering Group
Co-ordinating partnership of main enthusiasts, key players (eg landowners, planners) plus representatives of a range of local interests

Host
Organisation taking formal responsibility (often 'in association with' others)

Consultants
Specialists in many disciplines

Support Bodies
National and regional

Team Chairperson
Experienced facilitator

Team
Independent specialists from outside the area with range of skills and experience

Organiser
Architecture or planning-related consultancy, institution or non-governmental organisation (May be the Host)

Advisors
Local community and business leaders, planners, etc

Technical Support
eg. University students of architecture or similar field

Support bodies

National facilitator.
Charles Zucker, employed by the American Institute of Architects to help communities organise Action Planning events, speaking in London, 1995.

Action Planning events often benefit from being supported by a national or regional organisation. Some organisations, particularly in the United States, have institutionalised their support into recognisable programmes. Support can include:

- **Advice** on the most suitable type of event based on experience.

- **Stimulation** of interest by provision of briefing material and speakers.

- **Validation** of the event which can be invaluable in overcoming scepticism at local level.

- **Assistance** with practicalities such as Team selection (through maintaining databases of talent) or Team briefing.

- **Organisation** of anything from an initial meeting to an entire event.

- **Momentum** ensuring that follow-up takes place.

In exchange for providing anything more than advice, most support organisations will insist on certain procedures being followed to maintain quality control. These will vary from one organisation to another.

Most support organisations simply respond to requests for assistance. But some may be proactive, encouraging and even organising events. This is particularly the case in the early stages of developing a support framework which is normally done by organising pilot events.

"In many ways, the process has transformed the way that Americans shape community development policies and take those actions that most directly affect their community's growth or change."

American Institute of Architects, R/UDAT Handbook, 1992.

See page 86 for details of some support bodies.

Types of Support Body

- **Professional groups**
  Institutes of architecture, planning or urban design for instance. Some have a special unit for Action Planning with a co-ordinator and committee (called "Oversight Committee" in the USA).

- **Universities and colleges**
  Some have a special unit. More likely to be a sporadic activity of a Department such as Architecture or Planning.

- **Local government**
  Can be part of the work of a planning or other department.

- **Regeneration agencies**
  As part of the work of a development trust or other special agency.

- **Consultancies**
  Support may be provided by private consultants who have developed the expertise in house.

- **Partnerships of agencies**
  A special unit may be established by a group of organisations, particularly at regional level.

Requirements

Before getting involved in a local event, most support agencies will want the following information from the event's proposers:

- ☐ Nature of the proposers.
- ☐ Brief description of community.
- ☐ Statement of current problems and background.
- ☐ Objectives of proposed event.
- ☐ Budget estimates.
- ☐ Statement of commitment from local sponsors.
- ☐ Letters of support for the concept from various sections of the community.
- ☐ Statement of commitment from the promoters to follow up the event.
- ☐ Any helpful photos or other illustrative material.
- ☐ ....
- ☐ ....
- ☐ ....

Funding

Action Planning events can be designed for a range of budgets. But insufficient funds, for the type of event you decide on, can lead to a failure to generate the critical mass of energy necessary for success. Establishing realistic budgets and securing enough money – or support in kind – is therefore very important.

Value for money.
Action Planning may appear expensive at first sight, but the cost of getting it wrong can be astronomical (tower block demolition, London 1985).

PRINCIPLES

• Funding should come from as many sources as possible. This encourages commitment to a partnership approach from the start and avoids charges of vested interest. If single source funding is inevitable, the need for a validating body will be greater.

• There are many opportunities for securing financial sponsorship and support in kind, particularly if the event is enthusiastically supported by the community and is high-profile.

TIPS

• Think twice before doing an event 'on the cheap'. It is most likely to lead to bitterness and recrimination. It is better to have a shorter, well funded event than a longer, badly funded one. Always allocate funding for follow-up.

• If you find it hard to get enough funding and support, try holding a 1-day event first with a view to generating interest in a longer one later.

• To avoid resentment and/or manipulation, be clear and honest about what is being paid for and what is not.

"You shouldn't do one of these things unless you are able to follow-up for two to three years at least. Action Planning events must be the beginning of a process, not isolated events."

Jon Rowland,
Chairman,
Urban Design Group,
September 1995.

Sample Event Costs

Mid-range estimates for 5-day events with Teams of 8 assuming no support in kind.
Excludes cost of organisation and administration and assumes Team members are
unpaid. Adjust accordingly.

Item and assumptions	£ National Event	£ Local Event	£ Your Event
Evaluation visit (travel, expenses)	400	50	......
Reconnaissance by Chairperson (travel, expenses)	400	50	......
Transport (Team members)	1600	200	......
Accommodation (Team members, 5 nights @ £50)	2000	0	......
Venues (rent)	1000	500	......
Equipment hire	750	500	......
Publicity, advertising, stationery	800	600	......
Catering (Team @ £25 per day plus snacks for all)	1500	1500	......
Car/van/bus rental	200	160	......
Film and processing (40 rolls @ £7.50)	300	300	......
Typists/word processors (100 hours @ £4)	400	400	......
Report printing (1000 copies x 100 pages @ £0.03)	3000	3000	......
Debriefing visit (2 people, travel and expenses)	800	100	......
Revisit (4 Team members, travel, expenses)	1600	200	......
Follow-up (unspecified)	1000	750	......
Sundries (supplies, telephone etc)	1000	1000	......
Totals	**16750**	**9310**	......

Funding Sources

☐ Local and central government
☐ Local and national businesses
☐ Local and national charities
☐ Developers and landowners
☐ Development agencies
☐ Community groups
☐ Arts councils
☐ Professional institutes
☐ ....
☐ ....

Support-in-kind Ideas

☐ Hoteliers	Rooms
☐ Printers	Printing
☐ Consultants	Admin
☐ Property owners	Premises
☐ Colleges	Students
☐ Businesses	Meals
☐ Bus companies	Transport
☐ Local press	Advertising
☐ Residents	Lodgings
☐	....

Setting the stage. Banners help people to orientate themselves and provide a useful backdrop for photographs. (King Cross Planning Weekend, London, 1990.)

Section 3
Preparation

Administration

Good administration is essential. The event must run like clockwork or energy will be dissipated and the results will be poor. Whether the event is organised by paid staff or by volunteers the principles are the same.

PRINCIPLES

- Once a decision has been made to proceed, responsibility for all preparation tasks should be determined (see checklist opposite).

- Clear guidelines about the nature of the event should be produced so that everyone knows where they stand.

TIPS

- Don't set a date until you are sure you can meet it. Fast-track events are possible but having a longer lead time is normally more likely to bear fruit. Avoid holiday periods and major local attractions. Best to be 'the only show in town'.

- Be clear about the extent of participation. Don't pretend there is an open agenda if in fact decisions have already been made.

- Avoid being unduly influenced! You may be lobbied from all sides by people promoting their own interests. Make it clear that the event is open to all and that the process is neutral, not 'fixable'. Suggest people make their case at the event.

"The impact of the R/UDAT (Action Planning) programme on the (American) nation's cities is unequalled by any other design activity over the past decade. No consultant organisation has worked so closely with so many communities. No government agency has dealt with such a rich variety of issues. The breadth, quantity and quality of experienced talent in the R/UDAT process exists in no institution or in any consultant organisation."

**Peter Batchelor,
David Lewis,
authors,**
Urban Design in Action,
1985.

Typical Tasks

3-6 months before

- [ ] Establish Steering Group and Host.
- [ ] Decide nature of event.
- [ ] Approach support body and organiser.
- [ ] Secure funding.
- [ ] Secure support in principle locally.
- [ ] Decision to go ahead.
- [ ] Establish administration.
- [ ] Inform local grapevines.
- [ ] ....

1-3 months before

- [ ] Select Team Chairperson.
- [ ] Start information gathering.
- [ ] Secure venue.
- [ ] Fix dates of event.
- [ ] Prepare timetable.
- [ ] Invite Team members (letter).
- [ ] Contact speakers (letter).
- [ ] Book accommodation.
- [ ] ....

1 month before

- [ ] Reconnaissance visit.
- [ ] Start publicity.
- [ ] Send out invitations.
- [ ] Staff organisation.
- [ ] Equipment hire.
- [ ] Creche organisation.
- [ ] Refreshments organisation.
- [ ] Equipment assembly.
- [ ] ....

2 weeks before

- [ ] Advertisements in press.
- [ ] Make banners.
- [ ] Check insurance.
- [ ] Check transport arrangements.
- [ ] Send out briefing packs.
- [ ] ....

Team Chairperson Qualities

- [ ] Experience of previous Action Planning events, preferably as Team member.
- [ ] Leadership qualities.
- [ ] Sensitivity and ability to draw people out.
- [ ] Understanding of urban design processes.
- [ ] Ability to orchestrate action.
- [ ] Toughness (may have to ask someone to leave the Team or deal with troublemakers).
- [ ] ....
- [ ] ....
- [ ] ....

Reconnaissance Visit

One month before the event the Chairperson should check the following:

- [ ] Budget.
- [ ] Venues.
- [ ] Publicity.
- [ ] Printing schedules.
- [ ] Film processing arrangements.
- [ ] Information gathering progress.
- [ ] Briefing pack.
- [ ] Report format.
- [ ] Equipment.
- [ ] ....
- [ ] ....
- [ ] ....

Getting people motivated

Action Planning events are likely to be most successful if there is widespread support and involvement from the outset. Often this will require imaginative promotion because it is still an unconventional approach which people may not be used to.

PRINCIPLES

- All sections of the community should be involved, particularly all the key decision-makers.

- Local groups should be encouraged to get their own members involved but should not be relied on to do so. Responsibility must lie with the organisers.

- The event should be promoted as an exciting and enjoyable opportunity, not a duty. People should take part because they want to not because they feel they ought.

"This process allows the members of the community to take a proactive role in the development of their community instead of the reactionary role usually associated with public hearings and the like. Events like this are our chance to bring the community, the developers and the city, county and the state agencies also the elected officials together to formulate a shared vision for an area."

**Tom Bradley,
Mayor of Los Angeles,**
letter to American Institute of Architects, 20 June 1990.

TIPS

- Be prepared for some hostility from people who think they know it all and resent you treading on what they see as their patch. Overcome it by using past examples and talking through the process.

- Get out in the community. Local public meetings at an early stage can be useful for informing people about the process, identifying the main issues and interest groups and for stage management. Keep them as informal and open-ended as possible. Consider also a newsletter, leaflet, site office, advertising hoarding and any special communication methods appropriate to the specific community.

ACTION PLANNING NICK WATES

- Invite key interest groups and individuals by letter. Also make as much personal contact as possible.

- Style is important. Develop a lively, straightforward, friendly design style and encourage a casual yet professional approach from the outset.

- Don't be afraid to state clearly that the most effective motivation for involvement is enlightened self-interest.

- See also *Publicity*, page 46.

Groups to involve

- ☐ Friends and neighbours.
- ☐ Local councils, politicians and administrators.
- ☐ Planners and planning committees.
- ☐ Regional agencies and key staff.
- ☐ Chambers of commerce.
- ☐ Local business people.
- ☐ Community and voluntary organisations.
- ☐ Developers and real-estate professionals.
- ☐ Special purpose authorities such as housing and transport.
- ☐ Schools, colleges and universities.
- ☐ Environmental and civic groups and societies.
- ☐ Youth and senior citizens groups.
- ☐ Churches.
- ☐ Ethnic and cultural groups.
- ☐ Social and emergency services.
- ☐ Media (local and regional).
- ☐ Investors.
- ☐ ....
- ☐ ....

Inviting involvement.
Advertising hoarding and publicity leaflets (Shankill Road, Belfast, 1995; Anderson, Indiana, USA, 1985 and Blairs College, Scotland, 1994).

Team selection

Orchestration.
*Architect Richard Burton,
Chairperson of the first UK
Action Planning event
(Southampton, 1985).*

Selecting the event 'Team' is one of the first tasks of
the Team Chairperson and will shape the flavour of
the entire event.

PRINCIPLES

- Team size should reflect the scale and scope of
the event. Usually 8–12 members works well.

- Team members should have a range of skills and
interests tailored to the needs of the particular
community and the issues likely to be raised.

- Team members should be free of any real or
perceived conflicts of interest in the area or, if they
have any interest, it should be clearly stated.

- Team members should commit themselves to
attending the entire event. (People unable to stay
for the whole period should be advisors instead.)

TIPS

- Enlist the best professional expertise available
within your area of influence.

- Select people for what they know rather than who
they are, and for their ability to analyse complex
issues as part of a team. It is useful to have some
people who have been Team members before.

- Give all Team members specific roles (see table
right).

- Avoid people who are too similar. A balance of
sexes and a range of ages is essential.

"A heartfelt thank you to
the government and
councillors of Birmingham
for inviting me to their city
and so gracefully putting
up with my comments. To
ask people to come to see
you and then allow them,
encourage them even, to
be frank in criticism as well
as in praise is a sign of
creative spirit."

**Team member,
Highbury Initiative**,
Birmingham, 1988,
quoted in event report.

Team Roles and Responsibilities

Note: Several compatible roles may be taken by one individual.

Title	Brief	Names
Team Chairperson	Provide leadership, orchestrate event, take responsibility.	....
Team facilitator	Keep roving eye on group dynamics, reporting back to Team Chairperson.	....
Workshop facilitators	Facilitate workshops.	....
Workshop note-takers	Prepare notes of workshops in format suitable for final report.	....
Report editor	Commission and gather copy and illustrations. Prepare camera-ready copy.	....
Report subeditor	Subedit copy and assist editor.	....
Report production manager	Liaise with printer and photo lab. Coordinate graphic design.	....
Sound recorder	Tape key sessions and index tapes.	....
Diplomats	Liaise between different workshops to create linkages.	....
Photographer	Ensure key events are photographed (slides and prints). Liaise with photo lab.	....
Contacts person	Keep names and telephone numbers of useful resource people.	....
Follow up co-ordinator	Ensure follow-up takes place and publicise.	....
Slide show editor	Select slides for presentation.	....
Stage manager	Co-ordinate pool of people for errands etc.	....

Expertise Required

Skills and professional backgrounds likely to be useful on the Team:

☐ Urban design ☐ Planning ☐ Landscape design
☐ Property development ☐ Economics and finance ☐ Law
☐ Sociology ☐ Management ☐ Community development
☐ Architecture ☐ Journalism ☐ Ecology

Everyone, if possible, should be good at writing, drawing, organising, analysing complex problems, be in good health and be good at working with people.

Technical support

To provide back-up for the event Team it is useful to have technical support before and during the event. Although volunteers or paid staff can provide this, it is often better to involve local students of architecture or related disciplines.

PRINCIPLES

- Taking part in an Action Planning event can be a rich learning experience in organisation, planning, architecture, participatory processes, research and presentation.

- Students can provide a cheap, energetic labour force who will pass on the process to others. Students of architecture, planning and urban design are generally most likely to benefit and be useful.

- Within an initial time framework set by their tutors, students should be directed by the Team Chairperson or other delegated Team member. Tutor interference during the event can cause serious difficulties.

"It was like being back at college but I realised that there were 500 years of professional experience around the table. I came to the event as a cynic but left exhilarated. I have not had so much fun as a professional for some time. It recharged my batteries. When you hit the inevitable mid-life crisis in any project, having one of these events is a good way to give it a kick up the backside."

**Mike Galloway,
Director, Crown Street
Regeneration Project,
Glasgow,**
December 1993.

TIPS

- 3 or 4 students is enough to make a coherent workforce without dominating the event.

- Choose students who are energetic, keen, flexible, sociable, diplomatic and can take initiative. Wherever possible provide clear roles and briefs. Treat students as equal members of the creative effort, not dogsbodies.

- Encourage students to make a presentation of their experience afterwards.

Technical Support Tasks

Before the event:

- ☐ Gather background material.
- ☐ Generate publicity.
- ☐ Get to know the site and local people.
- ☐ Read this handbook and other material.
- ☐ Prepare exhibition and briefing for Team members.
- ☐ Prepare base models and plans.
- ☐ ....
- ☐ ....

During the event:

- ☐ Maintain a library of information.
- ☐ Service workshops.
- ☐ Act as personal assistants to the Chairperson.
- ☐ Take and collate photographs.
- ☐ Participate in all activities as much as possible.
- ☐ ....
- ☐ ....

After the event:

- ☐ Collate and store information for future use.
- ☐ Monitor effectiveness of the event.
- ☐ ....
- ☐ ....

Modelmaking. *Students from Moscow University preparing a 3-metre-square model for the ECO 1 Action Planning event in 1991. This became the focus for open-ended discussions with local people; problems and solutions being recorded on cards pinned to the model with cocktail sticks. A consensus view was thus established from which the design team could work.*

Information gathering

It is important to provide enough information for participants both before and during the event, otherwise the event will be spent gathering information rather than thinking out the way forward.

PRINCIPLES

- Selecting and presenting information is a central element of the Action Planning process and should be directed by the Team Chairperson.

- A briefing pack should normally be sent out to the main participants two weeks beforehand. Other material can be available at the event.

TIPS

- Use information that already exists where possible. Get key stakeholders to prepare presentations as this promotes active involvement.

- Start thinking about what will be needed for the final presentation right from the start. Collect data in the appropriate formats.

- Be selective. Too much information can overwhelm people and inhibit imaginative thinking.

- Set up a resource library and keep an index of useful material. Identify resource people to collect information on specific issues; eg: jobs, crime.

"The whole process was extremely creative. It brought a lot of people together."

**Ted Watts,
Past President,
Royal Institute of
Chartered Surveyors,**
December 1993.

- Think visual. Good photos, drawings, maps and graphs are more useful than wordy reports.

- Tie important reports and documents to table tops with string to avoid people mistaking them with handouts and walking off with them.

Basic Information Required

Not everything will be relevant on all occasions. Select what is and add anything else you think might be useful.

Maps, tables, reports and videos showing:
- ☐ Land use, transport and building condition.
- ☐ Political, administrative and cultural boundaries.
- ☐ Topography and ecology.
- ☐ Development plans and proposals, zoning and previous studies.
- ☐ Landownership, land availability and land valuation (including impact of over/under supply in the future).
- ☐ Population statistics and projections.
- ☐ Employment patterns.
- ☐ Tax information.
- ☐ Profiles of local organisations.
- ☐ Historical data: archaeological, protected buildings, area development.
- ☐ Tourist and area promotion information.
- ☐ Concerns and opportunities lists.
- ☐ Aerial photographs.
- ☐ Blank base maps at various scales.
- ☐ Information sources.
- ☐ Newspaper cuttings.
- ☐ Social profiles.
- ☐ ....
- ☐ ....
- ☐ ....
- ☐ ....

Sample Briefing Pack Letter

Dear

Anytown Action Planning Event

Many thanks for agreeing to take part in Anytown Action Planning Event as: (insert role i.e. Team member, Advisor, Admin staff, technical support).

A briefing pack is enclosed containing the following information for you to look at before you arrive:

- Mission statement.
- Team list with roles and responsibilities.
- Biographical notes on Team members.
- Timetable.
- Background material: (some of the material listed in the Basic Information Required box left).
- List of what else will be available during the event.
- Copy of *Action Planning*.

Accommodation and travel arrangements are as follows: (insert details with contact telephone numbers).

Payment and expenses arrangements are as follows: (insert details with any special restrictions on future commissions etc).

Please remember to bring your camera and any relevant slides or other material for the exhibition and presentation. Mark these clearly with your name if you want them returned.

I would be grateful if you would confirm in writing that the above arrangements are satisfactory and look forward to seeing you at (place) on (date).

Yours sincerely

Team Chairperson

Publicity

Media involvement.
*Planning weekend Host,
developer John Muir,
makes his case to the
television cameras (Blairs
College, Aberdeen 1994).*

Publicity is an essential aspect of an Action Planning event in order to generate a public debate.

PRINCIPLES

- Publicity is needed:
  Before – to generate excitement and ensure participation;
  During – to maintain momentum and disseminate the results;
  After – to monitor progress and ensure action is taken.

- The local media should be involved as participants in the process as well as observers. It is a rare opportunity for the media to play a part in generating community solutions rather than simply reporting problems.

TIPS

- Time the event to coincide with a political opportunity or a community event to provide added media attraction (but avoid distractions, eg World Cup).

- Put one person in charge of media liaison as part of a general information HQ.

- Maintain a comprehensive press kit explaining the issues and process. This can be the briefing pack (see page 45) with the addition of press releases on newsworthy developments and details of activities particularly worth covering.

- Try and get a special pull-out supplement in an established local newspaper. In addition produce a broadsheet including the programme.

*"The public is eager for
participation, elected
councils are searching for
new direction. Is Action
Planning the missing
ingredient?"*

**John Worthington,
President,
Urban Design Group.**
*Urban Design Quarterly,
January 1994.*

- Hold a press conference prior to the event and show videos or slides of previous events. Invite the media to take part throughout but particularly for tours, briefings and presentations.

- T-shirts, badges and banners can all be useful.

- Encourage local organisations to help with publicity by, for instance, writing letters to the local paper.

- Maintain a clippings file of coverage.

Creating a public debate.
Making the future of people's immediate environment news is an essential part of Action Planning. (Birmingham Post, 1988; Pittsburgh Press, 1988; Sunday Telegraph, 1989; Dorset Advertiser, 1989; Architects' Journal, 1990; Guardian, 1990; Southwark Sparrow, 1993; Shankill People, 1995 (a 36-page special issue prior to a planning weekend).

Venues

On location.
*Marquee used for workshops,
and an exhibition because no
large hall was available on site
(Poundbury Planning Weekend
1989).*

Premises which provide a stimulating atmosphere are essential. Four main types of space are required:

1 **Studio workspace** for the Team and organisers with lockable administration room, kitchen and toilets. 24-hour access essential.

2 **Large hall** for public meetings, presentations and exhibitions with toilets and refreshment facilities.

3 **Medium-sized rooms** for workshops, group meetings and a creche.

4 **Living accommodation** for Team members and organisers.

Ideally these should be next to one another and within, or close by, the area being studied.

"Action Planning events can change the way we plan because you focus on the area, you are in the area when you focus on it and you involve the people with a particular interest in seeing the area come to life. Normally you would be in an office framework, divorced from the site, and not in contact with the community that will be living in the environment that you create."

**Charmaine Young,
Housing Developer,
Wimpey Homes,**
December 1993.

TIPS

• Prominent venues on 'neutral ground' work best. Vacant shopfronts and schools can be ideal. Avoid town halls. Check venues are available for the whole period.

• It helps if all Team members and other key participants stay in the same place, preferably a good hotel with individual rooms (as people may sleep at different times). Late night bar and breakfast discussions can be very productive. Accommodation within easy walking distance will avoid endless logistic problems.

• Quiet outdoor space can be useful for workshops in warm weather.

Flexible space.
Six workshops taking place
simultaneously in a large hall.
The same space was used for
public meetings, presentations
and Team working. (Hulme,
Manchester, 1992.)

Good Room Arrangement

Room layout one might arrive at if specifying in the abstract.
In practice one has to improvise with spaces available.

workshop	screens	crêche		editing
workshop	large hall	kitchen	wc	studio	
workshop	exhibition	reception		administration

Fittings and services

The venues need to be properly equipped and serviced if the event is to function smoothly.

Workstations.
Flat-bed photo-stand used for photographing drawings and other artwork.
Below: Computers are used for making signs, leaflets, broadsheets and reports, as well as storing names and addresses.
(West Silvertown, 1993).

PRINCIPLES

- All work and domestic needs of the participants should be met for the duration of the event. People should be able to arrive empty handed and operate as efficiently, if not more so, than if they were in their own workplaces.

- Venues should be set up well before the Team arrives.

TIPS

- Self service catering with a constant supply of hot drinks and nibbles works well so that people do not feel bound by fixed breaks. But dinner can usefully be more formal to provide a change of pace.

- Rapid photocopier and computer repair service is essential. If in doubt have spare machines.

- Make sure heating systems can be made to remain on overnight.

"The community planning weekends were brilliant. People could really get to talk to somebody and get a straight answer. There was a nice atmosphere."

**Joan Maginn,
Chair, North Hull
Residents' Association,**
quoted in *Building homes people want*, 1994.

Fittings

Checklist for large-scale event with a
Team of 12. Adjust for smaller events.

Studio Workspace
- [ ] Chairs (office) and stools.
- [ ] Computers (see Equipment & Supplies checklist p52).
- [ ] Desks for writing (6) and for computers (4).
- [ ] Drawing boards or drawing tables (8).
- [ ] Drinks facility and fridge.
- [ ] Lighting, including desk lighting.
- [ ] Lock-up for valuable equipment.
- [ ] Pin board or pin-up wall.
- [ ] Photocopier (see Equipment & Supplies checklist p52).
- [ ] Plan storage system.
- [ ] Power outlets.
- [ ] Shelving and filing space.
- [ ] Table (conference) with seats for 16.
- [ ] Telephones and fax.
- [ ] Waste bins and garbage bags.
- [ ] ....

Large Hall
- [ ] Blackout curtains.
- [ ] Chairs – movable.
- [ ] Exhibition facilities.
- [ ] Flipchart (with non-squeeky pens).
- [ ] Lighting (friendly),
- [ ] Projection screens (2 large).
- [ ] Public address system with microphones on stands and roving.
- [ ] ....

Medium-sized rooms
- [ ] Chairs – movable.
- [ ] Flipcharts.
- [ ] Pin board and pin-up space.
- [ ] Table.
- [ ] ....

Services

Checklist for large scale event. Adjust
accordingly.

- [ ] Caretaking/reception to provide security for equipment: 24-hour.
- [ ] Catering: breakfast at hotel, buffet lunches, set dinners in a variety of venues, constant supply of hot and cold drinks, fruit and nibbles.
- [ ] Computer support (rapid, 24-hour cover on final night).
- [ ] Film processing: rapid throughout, 2-hour turnaround on final day for colour slides (mounted), 6-hour turnaround for black & white and colour prints (3ins x 5ins).
- [ ] Photocopier and computer repair service: rapid, 24-hour cover.
- [ ] Printers: briefed well in advance of scope of work and importance of deadlines.
- [ ] Telephone lines: two minimum.
- [ ] Transport: minibuses or coaches for Team tours and travel to evening dinner venues.
- [ ] ....
- [ ] ....
- [ ] ....

Equipment and supplies

A substantial amount of equipment is required to run an Action Planning event successfully.

- Support bodies may well have much of the equipment. Otherwise it will have to be borrowed, hired or bought.

- Equipment and supplies should be organised well in advance.

- It is better to over-provide than run out. Arrangements should allow for returning or reusing any surpluses.

TIPS

- Discourage mobile phones in the working sessions but they can be useful for dealing with press enquiries, suppliers and emergencies.

- Agree and standardise computer software. Prepare standard layout formats beforehand.

- Banners for the entrance, the main hall and workshops can usefully be prepared in advance.

Team Members' Luggage

- ☐ Smartish clothes for the start and finish.
- ☐ Casual clothes for the working sessions.
- ☐ Camera.
- ☐ Useful general facts and figures or illustrative material likely to be relevant.
- ☐ Material for special presentation if required.
- ☐ Any special favourite drawing pens.
- ☐ ....
- ☐ ....
- ☐ ....

"A successful event has to be as carefully stage managed as a theatre production – but one in which the audience and actors keep reversing roles."

**Debbie Radcliffe,
Actress and Team member**,
February 1995.

Equipment and Supplies

Checklist for large-scale event. Adjust accordingly.

☐ Banners and directional signs with fixings.
☐ Base maps and plans of the area at different scales.
☐ Blackboard and chalk.
☐ Base model with movable parts.
☐ Bluetak.
☐ Box files.
☐ Camera: (35mm) with wide-angle, telephoto, flash and close-up facility.
☐ Camera: Polaroid (for last-minute shots).
☐ Cardboard or polystyrene (for modelmaking).
☐ Catering gear: cups, plates, cutlery, napkins etc.
☐ Clipboards.
☐ Cocktail sticks (for use with model).
☐ Computers: 4 networked. One main server machine. Laser printer. Scanner if possible. DTP and word processing software. Discs and toner for printer.
☐ Compasses.
☐ Correction fluid.
☐ Cutting knives, mats, metal edge and spare blades.
☐ Dictating and transcribing equipment.
☐ Drawing pins, stick pins.
☐ Easels.
☐ Extension cables.
☐ Erasers.
☐ Filing trays.
☐ Film: colour slides for presentation, colour or black & white prints for report (20 rolls each).
☐ Film projector and screen (if relevant).
☐ Flat-bed photo-stand with colour corrected lamps (for shooting drawings and plans) and spare bulbs.
☐ Flipcharts.
☐ Food and drink.
☐ Hole punches.
☐ Layout pads (grid marked with non repro blue ink).

☐ Light box (large).
☐ Name badges (essential throughout).
☐ Paper: A4 & A2 sketch pads; A4 writing pads (lined); tracing (white and yellow); A5 note pads; flipchart pads.
☐ Paperclips.
☐ Paper trimmer or guillotine.
☐ Pencils: normal; coloured.
☐ Pens: felt-tips in bright colours and grey tones (different sizes); fiber-tipped with medium and fine tips (black and red); ball points (black and red); technical drawing (1 set); highlighters.
☐ Photocopier with enlarging/reducing facility (with rapid repair service).
☐ Photocopier paper, toner etc.
☐ Pointer for slide show.
☐ Post-its (different sizes and at least 4 colours).
☐ Pritt-sticks.
☐ Ring binders (A4).
☐ Rubber bands.
☐ Rubber cement.
☐ Rubbish bags.
☐ Rulers and scale rulers.
☐ Screen for copying photographs.
☐ Scissors.
☐ Slide projectors (carousel type) (2), with screens (2) and spare carousel trays (6), spare fuses and spare bulbs.
☐ Spraymount adhesive.
☐ Staples and staple extractors.
☐ Tape: masking, magic, heavy duty.
☐ Tape recorder and tapes.
☐ Toilet paper.
☐ T-squares, triangles and circle templates.
☐ Velcro pads.
☐ Video camera.
☐ Video play-back equipment (if relevant).
☐ ....
☐ ....
☐ ....

Team arrival. John Thompson and Team members disembark at
Aberdeen airport for a 5-day planning weekend at Blairs College,
1994, complete with boxed 'flat-bed photo-stand' as hand luggage!

Section 4
The Event

Timetabling

Launch. *Part of a leaflet
circulated before an event
(Hulme, Manchester, 1992).*

Skilful and imaginative timetabling is the key to
organising successful Action Planning events.

PRINCIPLES

- The length of an event should be determined by
the complexity of the issues and the resources
available but the structure will be similar in most
cases. Longer events normally span a weekend to
allow both professionals and locals to get involved
easily.

- Events are made up of a series of presentations,
workshops, visits, public meetings, working sessions
and social events. Some of these will be open to
everyone, others will be for specific groups only.

- The timetable should be determined and circulated
well in advance so that people can fix it in their
diaries and prepare themselves.

TIPS

- Short events – 1 or 2 days – may be useful for
relatively simple issues or small areas but don't
expect to be able to deal with all of the problems
of a city or neighbourhood in that time. Experience
shows that events lasting 4 or 5 days are
necessary for people to learn to work together
effectively and think through the issues.

- Don't let the timetable inhibit spontaneous
enthusiasm. The Chairperson should allow some
'unstructuring' and flexibility when possible.

- Allow plenty of time for relaxed meals; both buffet
and sit-down. Meals are a good opportunity for
speakers from local groups and for discussion.

*"The participation of
citizens in almost every
aspect of the process is its
key to success. The
process provides a
structured approach
through which citizens,
politicians and
professionals can speak
and listen to each others'
concerns and ideas and
raise the consciousness of
the community."*

**American Institute
of Architects,**
R/UDAT Handbook, 1992.

ACTION PLANNING NICK WATES

- Allow time for Team discussion on process; ie 'how to work as a team'. Encourage people to share their 'learning moments'.

- Keep people healthy by encouraging walking, swimming, and so on, preferably in groups. An intensive pace is essential but pushing people too hard can be counterproductive.

Timetable Structure

Note the common format regardless of length. Adjust to suit circumstances.

	5-Day Event		**1-Day Event**	
INTRODUCTION	Thursday	Tour of area for Team members. Briefings from key players. Launch event.	**Morning Session 1**	Introductions. Briefings from key players. Coffee.
PROBLEMS ISSUES	Friday	Open topic-based workshops to identify key problems and opportunities.	**Morning Session 2**	Discussion/analysis of key problems and opportunities. Lunch.
SOLUTIONS OPTIONS	Saturday	Open design workshops to explore future options. Team brainstorm over dinner.	**Afternoon Session 1**	Design sessions to explore future options. Tea.
SYNTHESIS	Sunday	Team analysis and determination of strategy. Report writing and drawing.	**Afternoon Session 2**	Drafting of notes on conclusions and next steps.
PRODUCTION	Monday	Report and slide show production. Exhibition/presentation to public meeting.	**Afterwards**	Production and distribution of report.

Sample timetable 5-Day Event Spanning Weekend

DAY 1   THURSDAY

8.00 - 12.00	**Setting up.** Room arrangements. Delivery of equipment and supplies. Erection of banners and signs.
12.00 - 13.00	**Team assembles.**
13.00 - 14.00	**Buffet lunch.** Welcome by hosts, sponsors etc.
14.00 - 16.00	**Reconnaissance.** By Team of area by bus/train/plane/foot.
16.00 - 17.00	**Political briefings.** By local politicians.
17.00 - 18.00	**Community briefings.** By local inhabitants.
18.00 - 19.00	**Technical briefings.** By planners, engineers, developers etc.
19.00 - 19.30	**Team briefing** . By Chairperson on Team working processes.
19.30 - 22.00	***Launch event.*** *Public meeting* and/or *dinner for Team, hosts and guests.*

DAY 2   FRIDAY

9.00 - 10.00	**Team briefing and preparation.**
10.00 - 11.00	***Setting the scene.*** *Presentations by local interests.*
11.00 - 17.00	***Topic workshops.*** *Open to all, punctuated by lunch and tea breaks. Several parallel topic-based groups, ending with a plenary report back.*
17.00 - 18.00	**Team review.** Detailed problem definition.
18.00 - 20.00	**Breather.** Minute writing, reading, exercise.
20.00 - 22.00	**Team dinner.**

DAY 3   SATURDAY

9.00 - 10.00	**Team briefing and preparation.**
10.00 - 10.30	***Report back on Day 2.***
10.30 - 12.00	***Lessons from elsewhere.*** *Presentations by Team members.*

Common Variations

- **Later start.** The American Institute of Architects favours a slightly shorter 4-day event: Team arrives Thursday evening for relaxed social. Reconnaissance and briefing on Friday morning. This can be more suitable for busy Team members.
- **Delayed presentation.** The final presentation can be delayed for a few days. But having longer to prepare has to be weighed against the loss of momentum and some participants.
- **Delayed report.** A popular option is to produce a broadsheet with a summary for the final presentation and for a small editorial team to complete the report over the next few days.

     ACTION PLANNING NICK WATES

12.00 - 17.00 **Design workshops.**
Open to all, punctuated by lunch and tea breaks and ending with a plenary report back. In parallel groups of 10-15.

17.00 - 18.00 **Team review.**
Developing central themes.

18.00 - 19.00 **Breather.**
Minute writing, reading, exercise.

19.00 - 23.00 **Team brainstorm dinner.**
Imaginative solutions.

DAY 4   SUNDAY

10.00 - 11.00 **Team preparation.**

11.00 - 12.00 **Team editorial meeting.**
Report and slide show structure.
Production strategy.

12.00 onwards **Report and slide show production.**
Writing, editing, drawing, slide making. Review meetings as necessary. Team only. Sleep and eat as and when.

DAY 5   MONDAY

07.00 **Printers deadline.**
Report and/or broadsheet to printers.

All day **Presentation preparation.**
Slide selection.
Exhibition mounting.
Hall arrangements.

All day **Clearing up.**
Tidying up, packing equipment and surplus supplies when finished with.

12.00 **Colour slides deadline.**
Final film development.

17.30 **Press briefing.**

19.00 - 21.00 **Public presentation.**
Slide show followed by discussion and formal thanks. Distribution of report or broadsheet.

21.00 - 23.00 **Farewell social event.**

Warning
Sample timetable not to be treated as a blueprint. Modify to suit local conditions.

Public Sessions
Sections in italics are advertised as being open to the general public. The remainder are for certain groups only. Normally the Team, organisers and technical support will be present throughout. Advisors will normally be present until the end of Saturday. In practice, events usually have an 'open' feel and people can participate as much as they wish at the discretion of the Chairperson.

Briefing

Action Planning events start with activities designed to provide the Team with a comprehensive overview of the locality and issues being dealt with. These normally include a physical reconnaissance and a series of short presentations.

PRINCIPLES

- Presentations should be made by all the main players so that the Team gains a rounded perspective; eg politicians of different persuasions, community groups, planners, landowners.

- Locals should take part as guides on the reconnaissance but the Team Chairperson should direct it to avoid it becoming a public relations exercise for sectional interests.

TIPS

- Presentations should be short sharp overviews. Don't let people waffle on and monopolise the time.

- Some people may prefer to say a few words during a meal break rather than in a formal meeting and this provides variety and interest.

- Tape record presentations for later use. Keep names and phone numbers of contacts who may be helpful.

- Viewing from a hill, high tower or helicopter/light plane is particularly useful.

- Everyone should wear name badges and introduce themselves as much as possible.

Briefings.
By local residents and specialists (Southampton, 1985; Poundbury, 1989).

"The basic notion is to get ideas which come out of the community's guts rather than ones which are imposed on them by remote authorities."

Patrick Harrison,
Secretary,
Royal Institute of British Architects,
Architects' Journal,
14 March 1984.

60

Reconnaissance.
*Viewing from the air, from an
open-top bus and on foot.
(Pittsburgh, USA, 1988;
West Silvertown, London, 1993;
Blairs College, Scotland, 1994.)*

Topic workshops

Topic workshops are a way of creating a relaxed environment for exchanging information and identifying key issues. They usually take place in the early stages after the briefings.

Menu.
Facilitator for a workshop on economics spells out the ground to be covered (Blairs College, 1994).

PRINCIPLES

- Participants are allocated to (or choose) a workshop. Each workshop will normally deal with a different topic; eg housing, transport, ecology. Team members are distributed evenly according to their expertise. Groups may vary in size but 10 – 12 is a good number to aim at.

- Each workshop needs a facilitator, notetaker, mapper (who marks points on a map or plan) and storyboarder (who summarises key points on a flipchart).

- A plenary session is held at the end where one person from each workshop (preferably a local person) reports briefly on the outcome.

"It was one of the very few occasions when you had the opportunity to see all the people who would be involved in something like that at the same place at the same time, and actually discussing things without discussing them behind closed doors in small groups. So it was a far more open process than you would get in any normal circumstance."

**John Barnard,
Acting Chairperson,
Barnwood Court Tenants
and Residents Association**,
December 1993.

TIPS

- There are many ways of running workshops. One way to start is to get everyone to write on post-its 3 things right and 3 things wrong with the present situation. Then sort into categories and review. Simple rules (eg no personal criticism) can be useful and should be displayed. Encourage Team members to take a back seat and let locals take the lead.

- Write up reports immediately to inform the next link in the chain. Use bullet points under standard headings: 'Who attended'; 'main issues'; 'proposals'.

- Keep attendance lists for reference later.

ACTION PLANNING NICK WATES

Sample Workshop Brief

Topic area: eg 'Housing 'or 'Transport'
1. What's wrong with existing situation?
2. What's right with existing situation?
3. What do we want (best hopes)?
4. How do we get there?

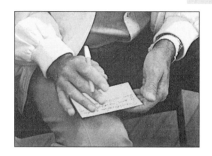

Topic Workshop Props

☐ Banner with workshop title.
☐ Large maps, aerial photos, etc.
☐ Pin-up area.
☐ Rules (if any).
☐ Pens or pencils (for all participants).
☐ Felt-tip pens (for storyboarding).
☐ Post-its (4 different colours).
☐ Flipchart.
☐ Notepads.
☐ Workshop brief.
☐ Standard report form.
☐ Attendance sheets (name, address, organisation if any).

Facilitation Tips

☐ Introduce yourself and get others to do likewise.
☐ Introduce session format. Ensure everyone understands task in hand.
☐ Steer discussion to ensure progress.
☐ Ensure everyone has chance to speak.
☐ Deal with any conflict.
☐ Wind up with summary of conclusions and next steps.

One method. Participants put their views down on post-its, which are sorted on a wall chart. The results are then discussed with key points recorded on flipcharts.
(Top and centre: Blairs College, 1994. Bottom: Wornington Green, 1989.)

Design workshops

Design workshops provide a 'hands-on' technique for allowing groups of people to work together creatively on physical planning and design. They normally take place after the main issues have been identified in topic workshops.

Summing up.
Participant explains workshop conclusions to a plenary session (Angell Town, Brixton, 1993).

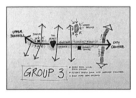

Output.
Summary drawing of one workshop's proposals (Shankill, 1995).

"The thing that got us about the weekend is that it showed that a hands-on approach to consultation really works."

**Justin Wilson,
resident,
West Silvertown**,
December 1993.

PRINCIPLES

- People work together in groups around a large map or model. Different groups can deal with different areas or the same area at different scales. Groups can vary in size (10 – 12 a good average to aim at).

- Everyone is encouraged to develop their ideas by drawing or making adjustments to the model. Each group needs a facilitator, a note-taker and a mapper (who marks points on a map or plan).

- At the start of the session, participants should choose which group to attend with Team members distributed evenly.

- A plenary session should be held at the end where each group reports the results.

TIPS

- Using felt-tips and tracing paper is often more suitable than using models because little preparation is needed. On the other hand flexible cardboard models can be very useful for helping people to visualise in three dimensions, and making a model beforehand can itself generate interest and enthusiasm. The 'Planning for Real' method can be particularly useful (see page 93).

- Get everyone to sign drawings at the end and draw up a tidy version for presentation.

Design Workshop Props

☐ Base maps.
☐ Tracing paper.
or:
☐ Base model with movable parts.
☐ Spare cardboard or polystyrene.
☐ Scissors.
☐ Post-it notes and cocktail sticks.
and:
☐ Coloured pens (different colours).
☐ Attendance sheets.
☐ Site photographs.

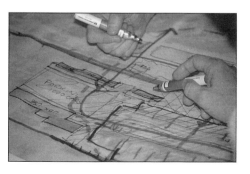

Hands-on. *Residents and Team members develop design ideas using felt-tip pens and tracing paper laid over a base plan. (Angell Town, Brixton, 1993; West Silvertown, 1993; Pittsburgh, 1988.)*

Meals and leisure

Doodling.
Sketch on paper tablecloth, made during a Team dinner, which was used in the final report and exhibition (Blairs College, 1994).

Mealtimes and other breaks can be made into a valuable part of the creative process as well as being therapeutic.

PRINCIPLES

- Mealtimes should be stage-managed to ensure maximum opportunities for informal and formal discussion.

- Leisure activities should be built into the event timetable to provide exercise, inspiration and opportunities for some social interaction and networking.

TIPS

- Invite local political, business and community leaders to meals which can end with brief speeches and debate.

- Organise dinners in a variety of inspiring local venues.

- Ensure that paper tablecloths are provided so that people can sketch on the tables during meals.

- An after dinner 'brainstorm' can be very stimulating, especially prior to the main Team editing session. Ask everyone to respond to 2 questions: 'What have you learnt in the past few hours/days?' and 'What are you going to do with it?' Have a flipchart at the ready.

- Saunas, swims, jogs, walks and a late night bar can all be productive.

"A bond was created between us. It was like sailing through the bay of Biscay in a great storm. I will be sad to leave. I had a very very good time. Buildings can be more economic if you know who you are building for. I hope very much that I can continue this work in Germany."

**Karin-Maria Trautmann,
Partner,
Trautmann Real Estate,
Berlin**,
London, December 1993.

Brainstorming. *Hilltop Team breather, and dinner for Team and guests, prior to settling down to report production (Poundbury, 1989 and Blairs College, 1994).*

Report production

The quality of the report of the event will be instrumental in determining what happens next.

Division of labour.
Report production roles (Poundbury, 1988).

- The report is a collective document of the entire Team. Who contributes what is not important. The aim is to clearly convey the Team's proposals and the rationale behind them.

- The report should be capable of wide distribution and of having a long shelf-life; it may be needed to reignite action in ten years time.

- The report should be completely assembled during the event and either printed in time for the final presentation or printed a few days later with a broadsheet produced in the meantime.

Editing suite.
Wall mounted storyboards allow everyone to keep track of progress (West Silvertown, 1993).

- A streamlined editing process is essential to produce the report in the time available. Establish clear editorial deadlines and responsibilities. It may be worth having a professional editorial team.

- Adopt a report structure and format at the outset, modifying them later if necessary. Stick to the main issues and be concise. Lengthy reports are unlikely to be read and are too expensive to circulate (1000 copies are normally needed).

- Assemble the report by pinning copies of text and illustrations on wall mounted storyboards. Keep originals in a binder. Get locals to proof-read to avoid misspelling names. Get Team members to sign the top copy of the report if there is any chance of controversy.

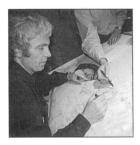

Drawing.
Working up design details (Berlin, 1995).

Sample Report Structure

Executive Summary

Introduction
Why the weekend was organised.
What happens next.

Background
Present realities, facts and assumptions.

Issues
Main problems and opportunities analysed.

Recommendations
What should be done (short & long term).
Who should do it.

Credits
Team members, sponsors, participants etc.

Sources and notes

Collecting Information Hints

- Three types of information are of most use; statements, quotes and images.

- Keep the report structure in mind when collecting information; ie everything should relate to a particular report section.

- Keep statements to brief bullet point paragraphs with one or two word headings.

- Record general identity of people quoted (eg 'tower block resident') or name and position in which case check it with them before using.

- All copy should have the following information at the top of each page: Originator's initials, typists initials, date, time.

Information Flowchart

How information is collected, synthesised and edited for the report

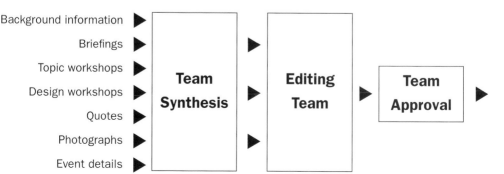

Background information ▶
Briefings ▶
Topic workshops ▶
Design workshops ▶
Quotes ▶
Photographs ▶
Event details ▶

Team Synthesis ▶ **Editing Team** ▶ **Team Approval** ▶

Sample Reports

Published reports are the normal way of refining and disseminating the recommendations arising from an Action Planning event, together, perhaps, with a broadsheet. Here are some examples of style and content taken from events on both sides of the Atlantic.

Examples from events in:
Anderson, Indiana, USA, 1985.
Pittsburgh, USA, 1988.
Theatre Village, Newcastle, 1988.
Poundbury, Dorset, 1989.
Wood Green, London, 1990.
Kings Cross, London, 1990.
Hulme, Manchester, 1992.
Helena, USA, 1992.
West Silvertown, London, 1993.
Burgess Park, London 1993.
Greater Shankill, Belfast, 1995.

Varied report formats. *From left to right: 24-page A4 printed document; 32-page newspaper; 122-page A4 photocopied spiral-bound document; 80-page A4 report on newsprint.*

Broadsheet distributed at a final presentation.
*An A3 folded sheet with the main recommendations, a vision
drawing and photos and summary of the process.*

Inside pages of reports.
*Note the generous use of sketches, diagrams, cartoons and photos
of the event as well as of the subject matter. A common feature has
become the use of quotations (mostly unattributed) from participants
in the page margins. Before and after photos and sketches can
also be very effective.*

Presentation

One of the most exciting and nerve wracking moments of an Action Planning event is the final presentation.

PRINCIPLES

- The purpose of the presentation is for the Team to present its proposals to the community and then to bow out, leaving the community equipped to take the process forward if it wishes.

- The presentation should be a public event with all those who have been involved particularly encouraged to attend.

- The timing of the presentation is fixed and advertised in advance to provide a deadline which cannot be avoided.

TIPS

- A good format is a slide show, preferably with 2 screens (to show before and afters) given by the Team Chairperson.

- Create an exhibition round the walls using flipchart sheets, post it panels, and other material from the event.

- After the show, get all Team members to sit up front, say a few words and answer questions.

- Conduct an exit poll to gauge the audience's immediate response.

- Make sure the acoustics are good.

Monday Evening
8.00pm

Report Back

The team will be working flat out on Sunday and Monday to turn all the ideas into a Vision for the future

See what you have helped create!

Exhibition • Slide Show

Don't miss it!

Deadline!
Part of an event leaflet (Blairs College, 1994).

"When I came in this evening I was struck by the sheer amount of creative energy and felt a sense of personal loss that I was not here for all of it."

David Lunts,
Councillor,
Final presentation, Hulme, Manchester, 1992, quoted in event report.

Sample Slide Show Structure

1 Brief history of the area covered.
2 Description of the Action Planning process.
3 Terms of reference for the event.
4 Run through of the event process on a day-to-day basis with conclusions drawn out at each stage.
5 Vision of what proposals could look like.
6 Summary of main recommendations.

Team work. *Sorting slides invariably takes place right up to the last moment (Poundbury, 1989).*

Reporting back to the community. *Exhausted Team members and hosts (front row) prepare to take the flak (or praise) at a public slide presentation of their proposals at the end of an Action Planning event (Poundbury, 1989).*

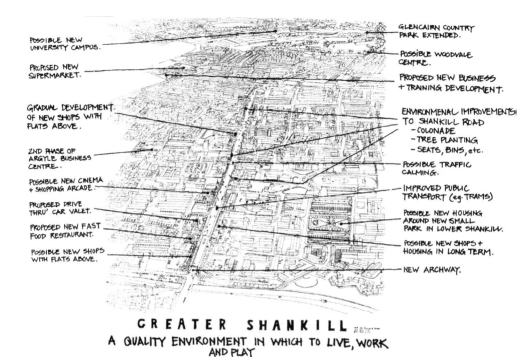

POSSIBLE NEW
UNIVERSITY CAMPUS.

PROPOSED NEW
SUPERMARKET.

GRADUAL DEVELOPMENT
OF NEW SHOPS WITH
FLATS ABOVE.

2ND PHASE OF
ARGYLE BUSINESS
CENTRE.

POSSIBLE NEW CINEMA
+ SHOPPING ARCADE.

PROPOSED DRIVE
THRU' CAR VALET.

PROPOSED NEW FAST
FOOD RESTAURANT.

POSSIBLE NEW SHOPS
WITH FLATS ABOVE.

GLENCAIRN COUNTRY
PARK EXTENDED.

POSSIBLE WOODVALE
CENTRE.

PROPOSED NEW BUSINESS
+ TRAINING DEVELOPMENT.

ENVIRONMENAL IMPROVEMENTS
TO SHANKILL ROAD
 - COLONADE
 - TREE PLANTING
 - SEATS, BINS, etc.

POSSIBLE TRAFFIC
CALMING.

IMPROVED PUBLIC
TRANSPORT (eg. TRAMS)

POSSIBLE NEW HOUSING
AROUND NEW SMALL
PARK IN LOWER SHANKILL.

POSSIBLE NEW SHOPS +
HOUSING IN LONG TERM.

NEW ARCHWAY.

GREATER SHANKILL
A QUALITY ENVIRONMENT IN WHICH TO LIVE, WORK AND PLAY

Dream or reality? Overall vision arising out of the Greater Shankill
Community Planning Weekend, Belfast, 1995.

Section 5
Follow-up

What next

The Action Planning process does not finish at the
end of an event. What happens next is vitally
important to ensure that the proposals are acted
upon.

PRINCIPLES

• Commitment to follow-up should be built into the
  process from the beginning and funding allocated.

• The nature of the follow-up will vary depending on
  local conditions (see box right).

• A definite programme and organisational
  mechanisms for follow-up should be included in the
  event report and announced at the presentation.
  There should be achievable targets and clear
  responsibilities.

• The local Steering Group, modified as appropriate,
  should normally take the lead.

TIPS

• Ensure that follow-up is the responsibility of more
  than one individual, preferably a local committee.
  Don't leave it all up to the Team Chairperson.

• Make the follow-up formal and publicise the results.

• Keep good records. Keep all videos, slides, tapes
  and press coverage of the event and send copies
  to suitable national bodies. Ensure that the event
  report is kept in print.

• Change the membership of the Steering Group but
  keep some continuity.

*"The process
demonstrated that urban
planning and design issues
can be clarified and
defined in a very short
period of time and involve
extensive and direct
community participation.
With continuing fine-tuning
and staff resource
support, it is possible to
move this programme from
its pilot status and
incorporate it formally into
the City's planning
processes."*

**Kenneth Topping,
Director of Planning,
Los Angeles,**
Report, 1 November 1990.

Follow-up Methods

☐ **Implementation workshops**
Organised by the Steering Group on a regular basis to monitor progress.

☐ **Team debriefing**
Perhaps 4-6 weeks after the event. Handful of Team members only if heavy travel costs involved. Evaluate event and assess next moves. Preferably in the host community.

☐ **Annual evaluation meeting**
Organised by Steering Group or others. Good for maintaining momentum.

☐ **Team revisit**
Handful of Team members revisit to:
a) Learn of achievements;
b) Offer additional suggestions;
c) Prepare an evaluation report.
Six months to one year after the event and then periodically at intervals. Visits can be formal or informal.

☐ **Newsletter**
Distributed on a regular basis with updated information on progress.

☐ **Report reviews**
Special meetings can be set up to run through the report with community leaders.

☐ ....

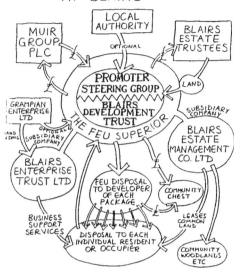

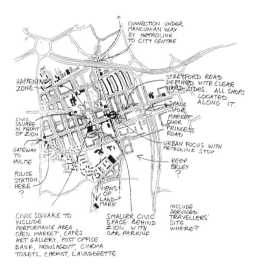

Ways forward. Diagram of proposed development process, and sketch showing urban design proposals, both drawn up at Action Planning events and included in the event reports. (Blairs College, Aberdeen, 1994 and Hulme, Manchester, 1992).

Evaluation

Evaluating the impact of Action Planning events is important both to help focus attention on long-term objectives and help improve the process. Start thinking about evaluation from the outset.

Implementation.
Sketch showing environmental improvements to a public open space, made at an Action Planning event, which have since been partially carried out (Southampton, 1985).

It will always be difficult to be absolutely certain that any change resulted directly from an event but do not be afraid to make an assessment.

The form opposite is designed to assist you evaluate an event. Try copying and completing it 1 week, 1 year, 5 years and 10 years afterwards. Get a range of people who participated to fill it in. Copies sent to the editor of this handbook would be much appreciated. Use extra sheets to elaborate but try and summarise in the space provided. Alternatively, make up your own form.

"The Wood Green event was an example of the new collaborations that are emerging....Our thinking on Wood Green and Alexandra Palace has been greatly enriched. Equally importantly, the enthusiasm both of Councillors and officers has been fired anew."

Nicky Gavron,
Chairperson,
Environmental Services,
London Borough of Haringey,
quoted in event report, 1990.

Common Event Defects

- ☐ Poor administration.
- ☐ Lack of information at the outset.
- ☐ Lack of interest by key players.
- ☐ Lack of involvement of key officials or other sections of the community.
- ☐ Logistical failures of equipment or people.
- ☐ Raising expectations without providing a means for them to be realised.
- ☐ Too much social activity deflecting Team from delivering.
- ☐ 'Noble champion' factor; lack of true team working due to one person trying to do it all.
- ☐ Team members being distracted by other commitments and not pulling their weight.
- ☐ Inadequate media coverage.
- ☐ Lack of systematic follow-up.
- ☐ Lack of adequate lead time.
- ☐ ....

Action Planning Event Evaluation Form

Title of event...

Nature of event..

Place...

Dates of event........................   Date of evaluation..

Name, title and organisation of evaluator...

Role at planning weekend (if any)...

Address ....

Telephone ....   Fax...

Summarise the impact of the event on the following:

Physical environment (buildings, parks, transport, design standards)............................
....
....

Economy (work prospects, wealth)...
....

Perceptions and aspirations (self view, hopes)..
....

Local organisations (changed roles, new partnerships)..
....

The participants (members of the public, Team members)..
....

How could the event have been organised better?
....
....

What would be your advice to other communities holding such an event?
....

Any other thoughts.
....
....
....

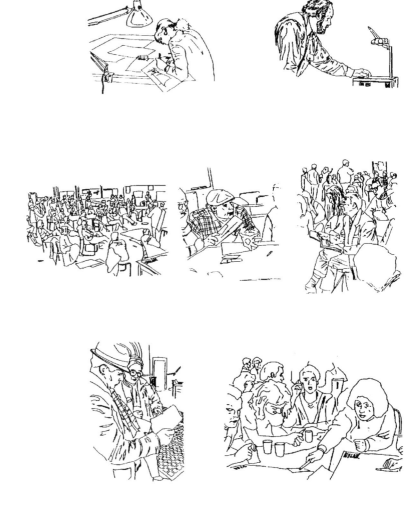

Work process. *Sketches from Hulme Planning Weekend, Manchester, 1992.*

Appendices

Potted History

1967 American Institute of Architects (AIA) responds to citizen in Rapid City, South Dakota, USA and sends a team of architects to look at problems facing the community. Programme of Regional/Urban Design Assistance Teams (R/UDATs) launched by AIA with an average of five events organised each year. Process improved with each experience.

1978 Similar programmes start to be evolved locally in the USA at state level by universities and colleges and by local partnerships including local AIA Chapters. These become generally known as Design Assistance Teams (DATs) although programmes have different names.

1980 AIA starts Generic R/UDAT programme to deal with problems common to many communities. Three events are organised over the next five years.

1981 Planning Assistance Teams programme started by US Air Force using R/UDAT process during weekdays to examine planning issues relating to its bases. 125 events held over next 10 years.

1985 First UK pilot event organised in St Mary's, Southampton by the Royal Institute of British Architects. It is called a Community Urban Design Assistance Team (CUDAT). Attempts to start a similar programme and support service to the AIA fail to get off the ground.

1988 Birmingham's 'Highbury Initiative' introduces 'think tank' style events to the mainstream UK regeneration scene. Handful of UK practitioners and community leaders take part in a joint US/UK team for a Generic R/UDAT in Pittsburgh, USA. It is the largest event ever held and is visited by HRH The Prince of Wales. This leads to a handful of events in the UK organised independently by those who took part.

1989 First UK 'community planning weekend' held at Bishopsgate in London's East End. Duchy of Cornwall hosts 'planning weekend' at Poundbury, Dorchester.

1990 American Institute of Architects produces handbook encouraging others to provide organisational support frameworks at state and local level. Over 100 R/UDATs and several hundred DATs now been held throughout USA. Urban Design Group organises its first event at Wood Green, London.

1991 UK consultants team up with German group and organise a 'planning week' in Moscow. Urban Design Group organises week long 'UDAT' in Pereslavl Zalessky near Moscow.

1993 Business in the Community organises its first event at Burgess Park, London. Urban Villages Forum organises its first event at West Silvertown, London.

1994 Urban Design Group announces intention to mount UK support framework.

1995   Action Planning Task Group formed by handful of national organisations to coordinate promotion and support services. UK consultants organise events in the Shankill Road, Belfast and at Hellersdorf, East Berlin.

1996   *Action Planning* published by The Prince of Wales's Institute of Architecture.

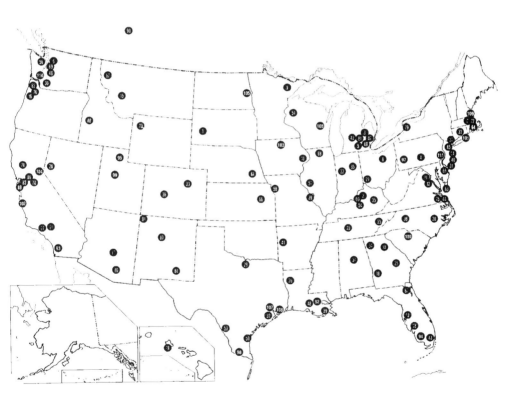

The American experience. *Over 125 4-day Action Planning events (R/UDATs) have been held throughout the United States under the auspices of the American Institute of Architects since 1967. Roughly half dealt with an entire city, a quarter dealt with the central area of a city and the remainder dealt with entire counties, neighbourhoods or open spaces. In addition there have been several hundred events organised independently at local level (not marked).*

Publications

A selection of material relating to Action Planning found useful in compiling this book.

Apart from some of the event reports, items can mostly be obtained from the sources shown in brackets or the organisations listed on page 86. Most material can be consulted at the library of The Prince of Wales's Institute of Architecture by arrangement.

BOOKS & HANDBOOKS

Building Homes People Want; *a guide to tenant involvement in the design and development of housing association homes*, Pete Duncan and Bill Halsall, National Federation of Housing Associations, 1994. Includes case study of community planning weekend in Hull. (from NFHA, 175 Grays Inn Rd, London WC1X 8UP)

Community Architecture; *how people are creating their own environment*, Nick Wates & Charles Knevitt, Penguin, 1987 (Polymath reprint 1996). Overview of movement for community participation in architecture and planning.

Creating a Design Assistance Team for Your Community; *a guidebook for adapting the American Institute of Architects' Regional/Urban Design Assistance Team (R/UDAT) Program for AIA Components and Chapters*, American Institute of Architects, 1990. Particularly useful for support bodies.

Creating Involvement; *a handbook of tools and techniques for effective participation*, Environment Trust Associates, 1994. Includes 2 case studies of community planning weekends. (from Environment Trust, 150 Brick Lane, London E1 GRU)

Future Search; *an action guide to finding common ground in organisations and communities*, Marvin Weisboard and Sandra Janoff, Berrett-Kohler, 1995. (from New Economics Foundation)

The Guide to Effective Participation, David Wilcox, Partnership Books, 1994. Overview of participation methods. (from Partnership Books, 13 Pelham Square, Brighton BN1 4ET)

Making Microplans; *a community-based process in design and development*, Reinhard Goethert and Nabeel Hamdi, Intermediate Publications, 1988.

A Practical Handbook for 'Planning for Real' Consultation Exercises, Neighbourhood Initiatives Foundation, 1995.

Real Time Strategic Change, Robert Jacobs, Berrett-Kohler, 1994.

R/UDAT Handbook; *a guidebook for the American Institute of Architects' Regional and Urban Design Assistance Team (R/UDAT) Program*, American Institute of Architects, 1992.

Tools for Partnership-building. How to build development partnerships between the public, private and voluntary sectors. In all central European languages and as a video. Compiled by Ros Tennyson. Prince of Wales Business Leaders Forum, 1994.

Urban Design in Action; *the history, theory and development of the American Institute of Architects' Regional/Urban Design Assistance Teams Program (R/UDAT)*, Peter Batchelor and David Lewis, North Carolina State University School of Design and the American Institute of Architects, 1985. Classic work, currently out of print.

MAGAZINES

Urban Design Quarterly
(from Urban Design Group)
No 28, September 1988. Special issue on Action Planning issues.
No 41, January 1992. Reports of events in Russia.
No 49, January 1994. Special issue on Action Planning events titled 'Involving people in urban design'. Articles by: Steve Bee, Jon Billingham, Anthony Costello, David Lewis, Jon Rowland, Alan Simpson, John Thompson, John Worthington and Charles Zucker.
No 58, April 1996. Special issue related to Action Planning.

THESES & RESEARCH PAPERS

Action Planning, John Worthington, DEGW Group, 1992.

A Community Participation Strategy in Urban Regeneration; *case studies in Muirhouse and Greater Pilton, Edinburgh and Hulme – Moss Side, Manchester*, Michael Carley, Scottish Homes working paper, 1995. Includes highly informative account and evaluation of a planning weekend. (From Scottish Homes, Rosebery House, 9 Haymarket Terrace, Edinburgh EH12 5YA)

Designing Livable Communities! *the UDAT as an urban design process*, Jeremy Caulton, thesis for Joint Centre for Urban Design, Oxford Polytechnic, 1992. Useful study on the transferability of the Action Planning technique from USA to UK.

Introduction to the Future Workshop Method, Reinhard Sellnow, shortened translation for ECO 1, Moscow, 1991.

What is a Community Planning Weekend? John Thompson, John Thompson & Partners, 1995.

EVENT REPORTS

A Case for Collaboration; *report of the Miles Platting & Ancoats Action Planning Team, 26-28th January 1995*. (from Miles Platting Community Enterprises, 2 Bradford Road, Miles Platting, Manchester M40 7EZ)

Cities don't just happen, *Wood Green UDAT; report of the Urban Design Action Team*, London Borough of Haringey, 1990. Good example of slim publication capable of wide distribution.

Blairs College Community Planning Weekend; *a sustainable settlement for Grampian*, John Muir Group, 1994.

Boise R/UDAT, Central section Idaho chapter AIA, 1985.

Central Avenue Study, Albuquerque, New Mexico, R/UDAT report, 1984.

Creating the new heart of Hulme, Hulme Regeneration Ltd., 1992.

ECO-1 International Community Planning Week, European Academy of the Urban Environment, Berlin, 1992.

Greater Shankill Community Planning Weekend, Greater Shankill Partnership, February 1995.

Internationaler Planning Workshop, Berlin – Hellersdorf, WoGeHe, 1995.

The Highbury Initiative; *proceedings for the Birmingham City Centre Challenge Symposium, 25-27 March 1988*, DEGW/URBED (proceedings of September 1989 event also available).

Imagine, Anderson, Indiana, R/UDAT report, AIA, 1985.

Last place in the downtown plan, AIA R/UDAT team, report of R/UDAT in Portland, Oregon, 1983.

The Newcastle Initiative; *Theatre Village Study*, Royal Institute of British Architects Northern Branch, October 1988.

Poundbury Planning Weekend, Duchy of Cornwall, (report and appendices), 1989.

Remaking the Monongahela Valley, R/UDAT report, AIA, 1988.

Report of the Burgess Park Urban Design Action Team; *29-30 January 1993*, Business in the Community.

St Mary Street, Southampton; *CUDAT report*, Royal Institute of British Architects, 1985.

Traffic management in Hastings Old Town; *an agenda for action*, Dr Carmen Hass-Klau, Dr Graham Crampton and Nick Wates (eds), Hastings Urban Conservation Project and Hastings Old Town Forum, 1989.

West Silvertown Planning Weekend, Urban Villages Forum, 1993. Good example of comprehensive report using DTP.

Addresses

Some contacts for further information and support on Action Planning.

American Institute of Architects (AIA)
1735 New York Avenue, NW
Washington DC 20006, USA.
Tel: 1 202 626 7300 Fax: 626 7365.
Contact: Charles Zucker.
Runs Regional/Urban Design Assistance Team (R/UDAT) programme as public service. Has samples of films, tapes, brochures and reports from US events. Supplies addresses of experienced Team members and local and state support programmes. Staff will visit and advise for travel expenses.

Association of Community Technical Aid Centres
64 Mount Pleasant, Liverpool L3 5SD.
Tel: 0151 708 7607 Fax: 708 7606.
Represents national network of professionals providing technical support to local groups. Provides training, consultancy and publications.

Better Towns Group
GKH-UDA 1, Design Works, Felling, Newcastle upon Tyne.
Tel: 0191 495 2495 or 0191 281 6981.
Contact: Gerry Kemp/Alan Simpson.
Emerging national programme promoting community-led assistance teams in small towns. Provides technical support and funding for project development.

Business in the Community
8 Stratton Street, London W1X 5FD.
Tel: 0171 629 1600 Fax: 629 1834.
Contact: Nick Thorn.
National voluntary sector organisation promoting corporate community involvement. Its Professional Firms Group promotes Action Planning and acts as broker of professional services to events.

Centre for Development & Emergency Planning
Oxford Brookes University, Gypsy Lane Campus, Headington, Oxford OX3 OBP.
Tel: 01865 483413 Fax: 483298.
Contact: Nabeel Hamdi.
General information on Action Planning, particularly in developing countries.

Civic Trust
17 Carlton House Terrace, London SW1Y 5AW.
Tel: 0171 930 0914 Fax: 321 0180.
Contact: Caroline Clark.
Regeneration Unit promotes Action Planning and may provide assistance with events.

Community Matters
8/9 Upper Street, London N1 OPQ.
Tel: 0171 226 0189 Fax: 354 9570.
National access point for community sector.

DEGW
8 Crinan Street, London N1 9SQ.
Tel: 0171 239 7777 Fax: 278 3613.
Contact: John Worthington.
Urban regeneration consultants with experience of Action Planning events.

Development Trusts Association
20 Conduit Place, London W2 1HZ.
Tel: 0171 706 4951 Fax: 706 8447.
National umbrella organisation for community-based development organisations.

Directory of Social Change
24 Stephenson Way, London NW1 2DP.
Tel: 0171 209 5151 Fax: 209 5049.
Publishes range of useful fundraising directories.

Institute of Advanced Architectural Studies
University of York, The King's Manor, York YO1 2EP. Tel: 01904 433959 Fax: 433949
Contact: John Worthington or Sultan Barakat (Post-war Reconstruction and Development Unit).
Postgraduate institute of York University specialising in 'Briefing for Conservation and Development'.

John Thompson & Partners
77 Cowcross Street, London EC1M 6BP.
Tel: 0171 251 5135 Fax: 251 5136.
Contact: John Thompson (formerly of Hunt Thompson Associates).
Consultancy in architecture, urban design and community planning with considerable experience in organising Action Planning events for the public, private and voluntary sectors in the UK and Europe.

MATCH (Managing the Change)
Knobelsdorff Strasse 10, D/14059 Berlin, Germany.
Tel: 00 49 30 326 5012 Fax: 326 5214.

Contact: Andreas von Zadow (formerly of the European Academy of the Urban Environment). Networking European agency, committed to sustainable development, promoting Action Planning.

National Council for Voluntary Organisations
8 Regents Wharf, All Saints Street, London N1 9LR.
Tel: 0171 713 6161 Fax: 713 6300.
National access point for voluntary sector.

Neighbourhood Initiatives Foundation
The Poplars, Lightmoor, Telford, Shropshire TF4 3QN.
Tel: 01952 590777 Fax: 591771.
Information and advice on 'Planning for Real'.

New Economics Foundation
1st floor, Vine Court, 112-116 Whitechapel Road, London E1 1JE.
Tel: 0171 377 5696 Fax: 377 5720.
Contact: Perry Walker.
Promotes community visioning, especially in the context of Local Agenda 21.

Nick Wates
13 Coastguard Cottages, Toot Rock, Pett Level, Hastings, East Sussex TN35 4EW.
Tel/fax: 01424 813970.
Editor of this handbook. Can provide consultancy on process management.

Prince of Wales Business Leaders Forum
5 Cleveland Place, London SW1Y 6JJ.
Tel: 0171 321 6474 Fax: 321 6480.
Contact: Ros Tennyson, Partnership Unit.
Organises partnership capacity-building events worldwide with focus on Central Europe.

Prince of Wales's Institute of Architecture
14 Gloucester Gate, London NW1 4HG.
Tel: 0171 916 7380 Fax: 916 7381.
Contact: Nick Wates/Suzanne Gorman.
Explores, teaches and promotes ways to improve the quality of the built environment. Publisher of this book. Can supply further copies; wholesale and retail. Promotes Action Planning through support of Tools for Community Design programme and coordination of Action Planning Task Group.

Prince of Wales's Projects Office
2 Hinde Street, London W1M 5RH.

Tel: 0171 224 1766 Fax: 224 1768.
Contact: Brian Hanson.
Coordinating agency for project development, community planning and vision processes. Organises annual European Urban Design Task Force.

Royal Institute of British Architects
66 Portland Place, London W1N 4AD.
Tel: 0171 580 5533 Fax: 225 1541
Contacts: Chris Church, Maureen Reed.
Community Architecture Group funds feasibility studies which may include Action Planning and co-ordinates Percentage for Participation campaign promoting user participation in building.

Urban Design Group
6 Ashbrook Courtyard, Westbrook Street, Blewbury, Oxfordshire OX11 9QA.
Tel: 01235 851415 Fax: 851410.
Contact: Jon Rowland/Susie Turnbull.
National voluntary organisation that helps set urban design agenda. Organises lectures, workshops, seminars, conferences and study tours. Promotes Action Planning. Maintains list of professionals willing to serve on event Teams.

Urban Villages Forum
8 Stratton Street, London W1X 5FD
Tel: 0171 629 1600 Fax: 629 1834
Contact: Gail Hallyburton/Harriet Price.
Campaigning organisation promoting urban villages; the planning and development of integrated, sustainable communities. Has worked with other organisations on planning weekends and can provide support for events. Maintains list of professionals willing to serve on Teams.

URBED
3 Stamford Street, London SE1 9NT.
Tel: 0171 928 9515 Fax: 261 1015.
Contact: Nicholas Falk.
Urban regeneration consultants with experience of Action Planning events.

Vista Consulting
140 Ryde Park Road, Rednal, Birmingham B45 8RF.
Tel/fax: 0121 457 8450.
Contact: Ann Brooks.
Information and consultancy on critical mass events such as Real Time Strategic Change.

Events Listing

Main Action Planning events held in the UK, or held elsewhere but with strong UK involvement.

Date	Name/Place	Nature
5/85	St Mary's Southampton	Inner city regeneration
3/88	Highbury Initiative, Birmingham	New vision for entire city
3/88	Mon Valley, Pittsburgh, USA	Redundant steel industry valley regeneration
10/88	Theatre Village, Newcastle	Central city regeneration
11/88	Maiden Lane, London	Modern housing estate improvements
1/89	Bishopsgate, London	Redundant railway land redevelopment
6/89	Poundbury, Dorchester	New settlement proposal
10/89	Wornington Green, London	Housing estate improvements
11/89	Old Town, Hastings	Traffic improvements in historic town
4/90	Wood Green, London	New vision for metropolitan district
7/90	Cape Hill, Sandwell	'Radburn' housing estate redesign
9/90	Kings Cross, London	Alternative plan for key inner city site
11/90	Smethwick, Sandwell	Inner City Renewal Area
7/91	North Hull, Kingston-Upon-Hull	Housing estates improvements
4/91	East Finchley, London	Redundant factory site reuse
5/91	Pereslavl, Russia	Provincial historic town planning proposals
5/91	ECO 1, Moscow	Metropolitan district planning proposals
8/91	Penwith Manor Estate, Lambeth	Housing estates improvements
5/92	St Helier, Jersey	Neighbourhood regeneration
11/92	Hulme, Manchester	Inner city regeneration
1/93	Burgess Park, Southwark, London	District park regeneration
2/93	Castle Vale, Birmingham	Vision for housing area on city outskirts
8/93	Angell Town, Brixton, London	Housing estate improvements
12/93	West Silvertown, London	Urban village proposal for docklands
4/94	Barcelona, Spain	Principles of sustainable development
5/94	Hammersmith Broadway, London	Inner city neighbourhood regeneration
6/94	Blairs College, Aberdeen	New sustainable settlement proposal
6/94	Muirhouse, Edinburgh	Housing estate regeneration
9/94	Rocester, Staffordshire	Housing site in village centre proposals
12/94	Turin, Italy	Ecological inner city regeneration
1/95	Miles Platting, Manchester	Inner city industrial area regeneration
2/95	Shankill Road, Belfast	Inner city regeneration
9/95	Blairs College, Aberdeen	Vision for university village proposal
10/95	Hellersdorf, East Berlin	Vision for system-built mass housing estate
11/95	Rochdale, Yorkshire	Mixed use canalside regeneration scheme

Eligibility. Events listed have followed fairly closely the process outlined in this book, or have been described as Action Planning events, planning weekends or urban design assistance teams. Many excellent but more general community planning exercises, including 'planning for real' events have not been included.

* Events held over more than one weekend.

Length	Host/Organiser/Chairperson or Coordinator
3 days	St Mary Street Group & City of Southampton/RIBA/Richard Burton
3 days*	Birmingham City & DoE's City Action Team/URBED & DEGW/Nicholas Falk
5 days	American Institute of Architects/John P Clarke
5 days	RIBA (Northern)/Newcastle Initiative/Neil Barker, Alan Simpson & JT
5 days	London Borough of Camden/HTA/JT
5 days	London & Edinburgh Trust/ Environment Trust & HTA /JT & Jon Aldenton
5 days	Duchy of Cornwall/HTA/JT
5 days	Kensington Housing Trust/HTA/JT
1 day	Hastings Old Town Forum/Urban Conservation Project/Nick Wates
2 days	Haringey Council/Urban Design Group/John Worthington
5 days	Sandwell Metropolitan Borough Council/HTA/JT
5 days	Kings Cross Team/HTA/JT
5 days	Sandwell Metropolitan Borough Council/HTA/JT
2 days*	North Hull Housing Action Trust
5 days	local Labour Party & youth group/Will Hudson
5 days	Cultural Institute for Independent Analysis/UDG/Arnold Linden
11 days	European Academy of the Urban Environment/Slava Glazychev/AvZ/JT
5 days	London Borough of Lambeth/HTA/JT
5 days	States of Jersey/Mason Design Partnership and HTA/Derek Mason & JT
5 days	Hulme Regeneration Ltd/HTA/JT
2 days	Business in the Community/DEGW/John Worthington
4 days*	Castle Vale Housing Action Trust/HTA/JT
5 days	London Borough of Lambeth/HTA/JT
5 days	London Docklands Development Corporation/Urban Villages Forum/JT
7 days	City of Barcelona/EAUE/Andreas von Zadow/JT
2 days	Hammersmith Community Trust/Vision for London/David Lewis
5 days	John Muir Group/HTA/JT
5 days	The Northwest Edinburgh Area Renewal/Vance Allen Associates
2 days	The Planning Cooperative/Ian Davison
7 days	City of Turin/Softech/EAUE/Antonella Marruco/AvZ/JT
3 days	Miles Platting Development Trust/Business in the Community/JW
5 days	Greater Shankill Partnership/John Thompson & Partners/JT
4 days	John Muir Group/JT&P/JT
5 days	Wohnungsbaugeselleschaft (WoGeHe) Hellersdorf/JT&P/JT
5 days	Rochdale Partnership/JT&P/JT

Abbreviations

AvZ	Andreas von Zadow	JT	John Thompson
EAUE	European Academy of the Urban Environment	JT&P	John Thompson & Partners
		JW	John Worthington
HTA	Hunt Thompson Associates	UDG	Urban Design Group

Case studies

Examples of Action Planning events indicating the impact of several different approaches.

Title, location, date and nature of event

Outcome

North Downtown area, Portland, Oregon, USA, 1983.
Standard 4-day R/UDAT organised by the American Institute of Architects to explore future possibilities for a neglected part of the central business district.

A new local business association was formed immediately and a follow-up policy report, based on the event's proposals for land use and transport, was adopted by the City authorities two years later. A local property owners' association was formed in 1986 which produced an improvement programme for historic areas. In 1988, a Downtown development programme released by the City stated that the event had 'stimulated considerable interest in the North Downtown Area which led to the establishment of several area organisations, and inspired further in-depth studies by the Planning Bureau.'

An evaluation in 1992 – nine years after the R/UDAT event - states that the event's report is 'still being used by city hall'. 'Individual developers now use the UDAT study regularly to interest investors in the area's potential…whilst the recommendations on transportation and infrastructure improvements are being actively pursued through collaborations between the city authority and community and business interests.' [1]

The Highbury Initiative, Birmingham, UK, 1988.
3-day event to provide a new vision for the entire city. Hosted by the City Council and funded by the Department of the Environment's City Action Team.

The proposals produced by the event were adopted by the City Council as a provisional strategy for the city centre. The event also led to the City Engineer downgrading the inner city ring road and giving pedestrians priority.

A subsequent event one year later led to the formation of a special council committee to deal with the city centre, the setting up of associations for different neighbourhoods and the appointment of consultants to prepare urban design guidelines for them.

An evaluation in 1995 concludes: 'The event succeeded in generating a new vision, shifting the agenda and priorities and enlisting new energy. The work of the City Council in transforming the centre, with for example extensive public art, has helped to stem decline and boost investment prospects, and has been widely acclaimed by those who have seen the results.' [2]

1. *R/UDAT Handbook*, and Alan Simpson and Charles Zucker in *Urban Design Quarterly* No 49, January 1994.
2. Nicholas Falk, URBED, letter to the editor, 24 January 1995.

Castle Vale Community Planning Weekend, Birmingham, 1993.
5-day event as part of an 8-week consultation exercise on the future of a 1960s estate of 5,000 homes on the city outskirts. Commissioned by the Department of the Environment prior to tenants voting whether to form a Housing Action Trust.

The event helped residents establish a strategic vision for improvements to the estate and was followed by the highest ever recorded vote in favour of forming a housing action trust to take over management from the local authority.

A second, 2-day, community planning weekend was held to develop a physical masterplan; testing out proposals from the first event and those developed by the architects to ensure that the masterplan was fully in tune with what both local residents and local officials wanted. The masterplan has since been adopted in its entirety by the Housing Action Trust.

Traffic Management Study Day, Hastings Old Town, 1989.
1-day event to resolve traffic problems. Organised for a partnership of local groups by a local urban regeneration project.

The event resulted in proposals for a range of traffic calming measures which had not previously been thought of and which were unanimously agreed by all parties. Shortly afterwards the Borough's traffic officer was sent on a traffic calming training course. Local residents established a special working party and campaigned successfully for, and helped design, traffic calming measures in one street. Another strategic traffic calming measure was undertaken by the Borough and the County Council.

West Silvertown Community Planning Weekend, London Docklands, 1993.
5-day event organised by the Urban Villages Forum to test the idea of establishing an urban village on redundant dock land.

The event Team supported the proposal and the event helped to galvanise interest. Specific design ideas were generated, some of which later found their way into the developers brief for the site. Funds were raised to help establish a local development trust. The event was also a useful action learning process for the Urban Villages Forum which has used the experience in projects elsewhere.

Greater Shankill Planning Weekend, Belfast, 1995.
5-day event to plan a vision for the future of an inner city area particularly affected by the conflict in Northern Ireland.

The event attracted 600 people including representatives from 62 community groups, 45 public, statutory and private agencies and 5 political parties. It galvanised the Greater Shankill Partnership, representing a wide range of local interests, to prepare a funding bid for a £27 million regeneration project which, at the time of going to press, has been shortlisted by the Millennium Commission.

Glossary

An explanation of the sometimes confusing terminology used in the field of Action Planning.

Action Planning
An approach to planning and urban design involving the organisation of carefully structured collaborative events at which all sections of the local community work closely with independent specialists from all relevant disciplines.

Capacity Building Workshop
Term used by the Prince of Wales's Business Leaders Forum to describe events organised primarily to establish partnerships between the public, private and voluntary sectors on development issues. Evolved from planning weekend experience. First event 1992.

Charrette
See **Design Charrette**.

Community Architecture
Architecture carried out with the active participation of the end users. Similarly Community Design, Community Planning etc.

Community Planning Weekend
See **Planning Weekend**.

Community Visioning
Term used to describe methods for getting communities to think and plan ahead.

Critical Mass Event
Umbrella term for relatively new organisation development technique involving large-scale events often lasting several days and often involving hundreds of people. Mostly used for organisational change but may also be appropriate for community planning. Labels given to specific types of event – structured in different ways and promoted by different people – include **Future Search Conference, Large-Scale Interactive Process, Conference Model, Real-Time Strategic Change, Participative Work Redesign** and **Open-Space Meetings**.

Design Assistance Team (DAT)
Term now used by the American Institute of Architects to describe state level Action Planning events. These evolved from the Institute's 20-year national level **Regional/Urban Design Assistance Team (R/UDAT)** programme (see below). Similar terms in use include **Urban Design Assistance Team (UDAT)** and **Housing Assistance Team (HAT)** (where only housing involved). Local **DAT** programmes have a wide variety of names; for example Ontario's **Community Assist/Urban Study Effort (CAUSE)** and Mississippi's **Small Town Action Team (STAT)**. First UK event was called a **Community/Urban Design Assistance Team (CUDAT)**.

Design Charrette
Intensive design session, often including 'all-nighter', originally just for architecture students but more recently including the public and professionals. Term originated at the Paris Ecole des Beaux-Arts at the turn of the century and is widely used in the USA. **Charrette** now often used without the 'Design' in front.

Design Day
Term used by the Royal Institute of British Architects to describe day when teams comprising architects and local people brainstorm for design solutions to particular building problems.

Focus Group
Small group of people who work through an issue in workshop session.

Future Workshop
Method for finding creative solutions for pressing problems using topic-based workshop. Not restricted to planning issues. Devised by Robert Jungk.

Participatory Rapid Appraisal (PRA)
Method for gaining a rapid in-depth understanding of a community, or certain aspects of a community, based on the participation of that community. Not restricted to planning issues.

Planning for Real
Technique for community involvement in planning and development focussing on the construction and use of flexible cardboard models and priority cards. Devised by Dr Tony Gibson and now promoted by the Neighbourhood Initiatives Foundation (see pages 84, 87).

Planning Assistance Team (PAT)
Event programme started by US Air Force using R/UDAT process during weekdays to examine planning issues relating to its bases.

Planning Weekend
Term most commonly used in the UK for an Action Planning event spanning a weekend. First used in 1989 at Bishopsgate. The term **Community Planning Weekend** is also used (often with the word 'community' being added during the process). Terms **Planning Week** and **Community Planning Week** have also been used for slightly longer events. Also **Community Planning Day**.

Regional/Urban Design Assistance Team (R/UDAT)
The first urban design orientated Action Planning event programme started by the American Institute of Architects in 1967 and still running. A **Generic R/UDAT** uses same process to look at problems common to many communities. A **Mini R/UDAT** uses similar process with a student Team. See also **Design Assistance Team**.

Stakeholder
Person or organisation with an interest because they will be affected or may have some influence.

Study Day
Day spent examining a particular issue. Often the programme is based on a similar structure to a planning weekend. Useful for simple issues.

Task Force
Term used to describe The Prince of Wales's annual European Summer School in Civil Architecture. An Action Planning process over a 6-week period with emphasis on education.

Think Tank
Increasingly used by governments and city authorities, often for 'experts' only. More conventional approach but may use an Action Planning format. Sometimes called **Expert Panel** or **Symposium**.

Urban Design
Emerging discipline concerned with the built form and ecology of streets, neighbourhoods and cities.

Urban Design Action Team
Term adopted by the Urban Design Group for its first UK Action Planning event in 1990 and used again since. (Note the American Assistance has changed to Action – see **Design Assistance Team**.)

Workshop
Meeting at which a small group, perhaps aided by a facilitator, explores issues, develops ideas and makes decisions. A less formal and more creative counterpart to public meetings and committees. A **Topic Workshop** focusses on specific issues. A **Design Workshop** includes the use of participatory design techniques.

Action Planning Planner

An aid to designing your own event.

	Sample (based on example page 27)
Location	Anytown.
Reason for Action Planning	Decline of traditional industry. Lack of investment in housing. Unemployment. Derelict sites. Uncertainty. Despondency.
Aims of initiative	New sense of vision. Programmes of action, long and short term. Agenda 21 response.
Type of event	Planning weekend.
Length of event	4 days.
Lead time	5 months.
Timing of event	Weekend before Easter next year.
Related initiatives	Agenda 21 conference. Developers' deadline for town centre.
Organiser	Anytown Environment Network.
Associate organisers	National Urban Trust.
Supporters	Anytown Council & Chamber of Commerce.
Approximate cost	£20,000.
Funding sources	Shell, Greenpeace, local firms.
Administration	Architects Company.
Support bodies	National Urban Trust.
Technical support team	Anytown College Urban Design Department.
Team Chairperson	Sally Facilitator.
Team members	John Engineer, Jane Ecologist, Simon Urbanist, Jenny Economist, Mark Editor.
Follow-up responsibility	Anytown Environment Network.
Other	Possibility of link-up with the government's urban design campaign.

	Your event
Location	....
Reason for Action Planning	....
	....
	....
Aims of initiative	....
	....
Type of event	....
Length of event	....
Lead time	....
Timing of event	....
Related initiatives	....
	....
Organiser	....
Associate organisers	....
Supporters	....
Approximate cost	....
Funding sources	....
Administration	....
Support bodies	....
Technical support team	....
Team Chairperson	....
Team members	....
	....
Follow-up responsibility	....
Other	....
	....

The Editor

Nick Wates is a writer, researcher and publisher specialising in community-based planning and architecture.

Previous books include *The Battle for Tolmers Square*, Routledge, 1976 and *Community Architecture; how people are creating their own environment* (with Charles Knevitt), Penguin, 1987 (also in Japanese, 1992, and Chinese, 1993).

Since his first involvement with Action Planning in 1985, he has participated in eight events in the roles of journalist, coordinator, Team member, support staff and observer.

He is a Senior Research Associate at The Prince of Wales's Institute of Architecture in London and lives on the south coast of England between Hastings and Rye.